THE GREAT
· WAR DIARIES ·

THE GREAT
· WAR DIARIES ·

ACCOMPANIES THE ASTONISHING
BBC TV SERIES

GUNNAR & FLORIAN DEDIO

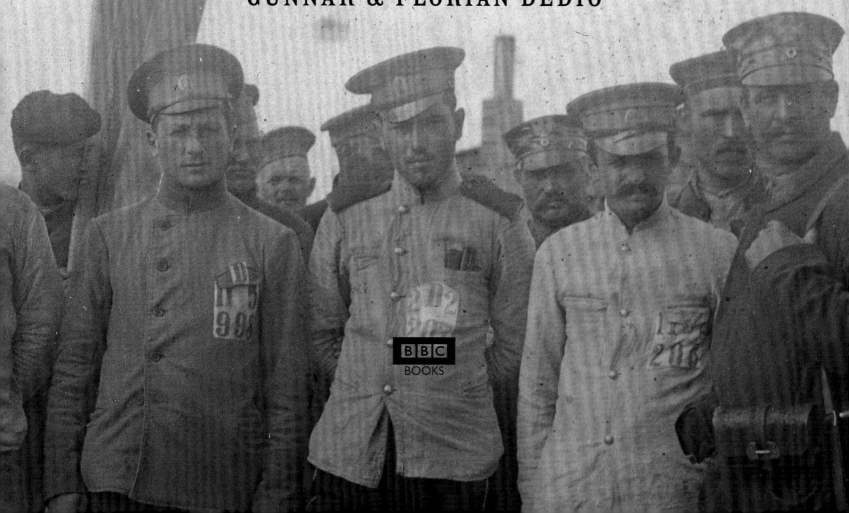

BBC
BOOKS

CONTENTS

FOREWORD

The First World War is possibly the most cataclysmic event in the history of Europe since the fall of Western Rome. What happened during the years 1914–1918 left its indelible mark on the whole twentieth century. You could say it was the original disaster from which all others trace their origins. Without the First World War the Bolsheviks would never have become the rulers of Russia, and the Nazis would never have risen to power in Germany; there would have been no Second World War, and no Holocaust, and no Cold War either.

The passions that once made the First World War possible are gone now. In one sense this allows for a deeper understanding that was difficult and perhaps even impossible before, when these energies were alive. But this also means that something important tends to elude us, making our remembrance more and more intellectual. And at the same time the spectre of anachronism looms: it is well nigh impossible to really understand the First World War, without insights in the contemporary psyche.

The participants themselves entertained a number of often sharply conflicting images of what the war really was: a crusade, an adventure, a pointless butchery, etc. It is not even uncommon to find these conflicting images inside a single person. Because what we might call 'the contemporary psyche' is of course a very complicated thing. And here I want to quote Frederic Manning, who wrote one of the most insightful books that came out of the First World War, *Her Privates We*:

> *"There was no man of them unaware of the mystery which encompassed him, for he was a part of it; he could neither separate himself entirely from it, nor identify himself with it completely. A man might rave against war; but war, from among its myriad faces, could always turn towards him one, which was his own."*

This book is indeed a book of myriad faces, not concentrating on the drama of war but instead focusing on the everyday experience, and by doing so telling us something essential about the multiplicity of war. Seeing all these faces, and reading their testimonies, makes it impossible for us to dismiss what happened to them using some simple formulae; the conflicting images persist. Like the passions that once intoxicated them or tormented them, the people you will meet in this book are themselves all gone now, but something of them and of the event is still present inside us. For better and for worse.

Peter Englund

ABOUT THIS BOOK

During research for our film production commemorating the centenary of the First World War, we stumbled across the photographic collection of German photographer and entrepreneur August Fuhrmann. It contained thousands of 3-D photographs taken all over the world between 1880 and 1918, many of them images from the First World War. The photographs – glass positives in 170mm x 80mm format – had been coloured by porcelain painters using a secret method that Fuhrmann never revealed. Despite being one of the most renowned photographers back in 1900, both he and his collection of photographs faded into obscurity after the First World War.

A few thousand of the glass plates survived in the care of a dentist in Warnemünde, a German spa town on the Baltic Sea coast, where they were used as a means of keeping child patients calm. From there, the plates made their way to the warehouse of the Cultural History Museum in Rostock, where they waited decades to be rediscovered.

In preparation for filming, we read extracts from over 1,000 diaries, letters and memoirs of men, women and children from all the nations involved in the war. We wanted to find out how it felt to experience the conflict from different viewpoints: as a mother, son, father, lover, soldier or nurse. We selected quotes from these eyewitnesses to include in this volume, and feel that they give every photograph an additional emotional dimension.

After the outbreak of war, August Fuhrmann's photographs are predictably limited to the viewpoint of the Central Powers. However, since this book is not purely about Fuhrmann's work, but rather about the First World War, we have included some photographs taken from other – Allied – sources in order to depict the most important moments of the war and the fates of soldiers on both sides.

We were particularly moved by the stories of English soldier and war reporter C.E. Montague, of Scottish nurse Sarah Macnaughtan, the German soldiers and poets Gerrit Engelke and Ernst Toller, the Austrian prisoner of war Karl Kasser and the French soldiers Alexandre Jacqueau and Maurice Aupetit. While we encounter other voices only briefly, we found ourselves living the four years of the war through these individuals' eyes.

Alongside the voices taken from diaries or letters, we have also supplemented each photograph with explanatory historical facts. Travel through time with us into the hearts and minds of our forefathers. One hundred years ago, they changed our world forever with the Great War.

Gunnar & Florian Dedio, autumn 2013

PREPARING FOR WAR

"Before a storm discharges itself with thunder and lightning, very particular processes occur in the atmosphere. The electric currents part, and the storm is the result of a certain atmospheric tension that can no longer be contained…"

Ottokar Czernin, Foreign Minister of Austria-Hungary during the First World War

On 20 September 1897, the ocean liner *Kaiser Wilhelm der Grosse* arrived in Southampton to pick up passengers for her first transatlantic voyage. A vast crowd of people had gathered at the dock to greet the ship with cheers and brass-band music. The liner belonged to the North German Lloyd shipping company and was the first luxury liner to be built in German rather than English shipyards. On 5 May 1898 the London *Daily Chronicle* reported that the *Kaiser Wilhelm der Grosse* had won the Blue Riband, the accolade awarded to the fastest passenger liner to regularly cross the Atlantic. The German Reichstag had passed the First Fleet Act on 28 March 1898, so the naval arms race began and Britain became Germany's opponent.

Albert Ballin, general director of the Hamburg-America line, rose to the challenge and ordered

Part of the so-called 'Rigi Bridge' in Switzerland. Before the war, people can travel across Europe without visas or passports.

the construction of the passenger ship *Deutschland*, which was launched on 10 January 1900. On her maiden voyage to New York, *Deutschland* received the Blue Riband. The two fastest passenger ships in the world, therefore, had both come from German shipping companies and shipyards. With further records achieved by the

Kronprinz Wilhelm and *Kaiser Wilhelm II* – both North German Lloyd vessels – the Blue Riband was retained by German shipping companies until 1907. Then, with the help of a loan from the British government, the Cunard Line built two ships which brought the Riband back to Britain. The *Lusitania* was launched on 7 June 1906, followed three months later by her sister ship the *Mauretania*. In October 1907, the *Lusitania* completed the Atlantic route in record time. Two years later, the *Mauretania* took the lead – and kept it too, for the 1912 maiden voyage of the *Titanic* ended in catastrophe. In the world war that followed, the most important factor in an Atlantic crossing was no longer speed, but safety.

In the battle of the passenger ships, no one had thought of using military might on the seas. But this had been looming for a long time on the European mainland. The relationship between Germany and

A stretch of railway line in the Alps. In the fifty years leading up to the First World War the railway has conquered almost every corner of Europe.

France had been poisoned since the Franco-Prussian War of 1870–71, when the German Reich was founded, somewhat ironically, in the Hall of Mirrors at the Palace of Versailles. Large parts of Alsace-Lorraine were annexed at that time. After that, the statue representing the city of Strasbourg on the Place de la Concorde in Paris was covered with a black veil which wasn't removed until 1918.

But France and Germany were not the focal point when it came to crises on the continent. The most intense conflict was playing out in the Balkans, from 1875, with some interruptions, until 1914. The first Balkan crisis was brought to an end in Berlin. Invited there by Bismarck, representatives of the warring parties and European powers came to the German capital in 1878 and decreed complete, or at least substantial, autonomy from the Ottoman Empire for Romania, Serbia, Montenegro and Bulgaria. The numerous subsequent crises and battles

Inhabitants of the Romanian village of Pistolati in front of their church. Before the war Romania is ruled by a Hohenzollern king of German descent.

in the Balkans were also negotiated and ended with the involvement of the Reich government. It wasn't until the Balkan crisis of July 1914 that war in Europe became inevitable.

In the decades following 1871, relations between the European powers were never predominantly hostile. Germany and Britain, for example, also had common interests. In 20 October 1913, they agreed to divide up the Portuguese colonies between them. Two days before, on 18 October, Austria-Hungary had delivered Serbia with an ultimatum after its occupation of Albania. But in 1913, Germany and Britain did not yet see any reason to become involved in the negotiations surrounding events in the Balkans.

Civic life in the European states was shaped far less by the military than by a mostly prosperous economy, international trade and a blossoming of the arts and sciences. Students from all over the world were studying at German universities, and their lecturers were bringing Nobel Prizes home to Germany each year. Grand department stores like Harrods in London or the Wertheim Warenhaus in Berlin were evidence of wealth and affluence, and were 'bombarded by a constant stream of bustling customers and clunking automobiles,' as the sociologist Paul Göhre wrote in 1907.

The military did, however, play a significant role in all European states, though it seemed as though its main function was to entertain the public. 'Military pomp and circumstance' made a significant impression at one of the greatest spectacles of the pre-war era, the Diamond Jubilee of Queen Victoria in London in 1897. The queen was accompanied on her route from Buckingham Palace to St Paul's Cathedral by 50,000 soldiers in parade uniform. Military choirs marched alongside as the sun shone down, glinting on the soldiers' weapons, horses' harnesses and artillery rifles as they moved through the streets. In Germany, schoolchildren would get the day off in order to be able to watch soldiers march from their barracks to manoeuvres. Moritz Bromme wrote of how the children watched in open-mouthed awe as the soldiers marched along in their resplendent uniforms carrying their weapons.

Only a few pacifists declared this military spectacle to be an omen of bloody carnage. Even the Prussian 'Junkers', wrote the British author and future Nobel Peace Prize laureate Norman Angell, were no longer regarded as fanatics, but rather as academics. The ships of all nations transported the freight of all nations, and all over the world automobiles were powered by spark plugs from Bosch and petroleum from German-British oil companies. As early as 1909, Norman Angell calculated that a war would lead to widespread ruin for both the victorious and the defeated. By 1913, his book *The Great Illusion* had been reprinted ten times and translated into French, German, Italian and Russian.

Romanian peasants before the war. King Ferdinand leads his people into an alliance with the Entente rather than with Germany – with disastrous results for his country.

He was supported by German social democrats such as Karl Kautsky as well as by German and British investors who, in 1914, collectively acquired oil rights for the territory which is now Iraq.

This time of peace also seemed to encourage close relations between the dynasties. Kaiser Wilhelm II was closely related to the tsars of Russia, and even more closely to the British royal family. He regularly exchanged letters in English with his close confidant Tsar Nicholas. Queen Victoria was Wilhelm's grandmother; as a child, he had spent a great deal of time with her. When Wilhelm's uncle King Edward VII was carried to his grave in 1910, Aga Khan, the Imam of the Ismailis, commented on how intimate the bond between the British royal family and Kaiser Wilhelm was. For in the funeral procession, Wilhelm walked directly next to the heir to the throne, George V. This led to a protest from Spain; King Alfonso XIII, as the oldest monarch, laid claim to that place in the procession. But Wilhelm was walking not as a monarch, but as a member of the bereaved family, as the Royal Family told the Spanish government in justification. Crown Prince Wilhelm of Prussia then took part in the subsequent coronation celebrations for King George V, sitting at Queen Mary's right-hand side during festivities in Covent Garden.

In June 1914, numerous British warships appeared at the Kiel Week sailing event. British and German officers and crews paid each other on-board visits. Sir Horace Rumbold, then an attaché at the British Embassy in Berlin, reported back to London that he had been greatly impressed by the warmth between the seamen of the two nations. The Kaiser was there too, with his yacht *Meteor V*. On account of his close relations with Britain, he was also an admiral of the Royal Navy. When he climbed aboard the battleship *King George V*, therefore, he was the highest-ranking British officer on the vessel.

British infantry crosses a river on the way to Pretoria during the Boer War in 1901. The Boers, equipped with modern weapons, managed at least to cause considerable problems for the apparently superior British Empire.

However, it had already become clear back in 1908 that the Kaiser and his relatives in Britain were not all that mattered when it came to Anglo-German relations. A report in the *Daily Telegraph* about a conversation between the British Army's Colonel Stuart-Mortley and Wilhelm led to a scandal in Germany. The Kaiser had expressed his desire for a rapprochement with Britain, with the result that the German press went on the attack, accusing him of trying to conduct unconstitutional foreign affairs behind the government's back. After that, the Kaiser was forced to keep out of such matters and respect the authority of the German Foreign Office.

On 29 June 1914, during Kiel Week, the Kaiser received a telegram informing him of the murder of the Austrian heir to the throne. The sailing regatta was cancelled and the seamen of the British and German battleships parted ways, becoming enemies from that moment on. Kaiser Wilhelm told his cousin on the throne

Japanese infantry during the Russo-Japanese war in 1905. Russia suffers a harsh defeat followed by a revolution, and by the beginning of the First World War is suffering from the consequences of both.

in London that he was surrendering his title as admiral of the Royal Navy.

One of the first German naval losses was the record-breaking ship *Kaiser Wilhelm der Grosse*, on 26 August 1914, when she was deployed as an auxiliary cruiser of the war fleet. She was sunk off the western coast of Africa by the British cruiser *Highflyer*. It seemed like revenge when, on 7 May 1915, the Blue Riband-winning *Lusitania* was torpedoed by the German submarine *U-20*. Of the 1,959 passengers on board, 1,198 perished.

In the period before the war, Fuhrmann's Kaiserpanoramas were concerned with two main themes – travel photographs from around the world and images of Kaiser Wilhelm II and the German aristocracy. Both themes embodied worlds that seemed far out of reach for the general population.

◀ **Trattenbach, Austria-Hungary, before the war.** A village like a thousand others in the 'Austro-Hungarian monarchy', as the Habsburg Emperor officially calls his Reich. His 53 million subjects speak more than a dozen different languages.

"Before a storm discharges itself with thunder and lightning, very particular processes occur in the atmosphere. The electric currents part, and the storm is the result of a certain atmospheric tension that can no longer be contained; whether we are able to recognize these processes in outward signs or not, whether the clouds seem more or less threatening to us, does nothing to alter the fact that the electrical tension must exist before the storm breaks. In the palaces of the Foreign Offices, the political barometer has been set to 'storm' for years. It rose for a while before falling recently, it vacillated – of course – but for years, everything suggested that world peace was endangered."

Ottokar Czernin, Foreign Minister of Austria-Hungary during the First World War

Berlin, Germany, before the war. The Siegessäule, or Victory Column, in the middle of Berlin proudly commemorates three military victories by the Germans: over Denmark in 1864, over Austria in 1866 and over France in 1871. The statue of Victory bears the features of Victoria, Princess Royal, then Crown Princess of Prussia.

"Then came the war in 1866, and for the first time I experienced the mass agitation that accompanied the departure of the fighters for the Fatherland; three times in my lifetime, in 1866, 1870 and 1914, filled with great enthusiasm. Oh! had one only been able to experience those cheers, that bliss, that floral rapture of the victory procession that I was able to watch in 1866 and 1871. For all eternity, the year 1918 ripped a hole in the German heart and German history, one that no ocean of tears or blood, only black ribbon after black ribbon can fill."

Carl Ludwig Schleich, German doctor

Constantinople, Ottoman Empire, before the war.
The fountain in front of the Hagia Sophia Mosque in Constantinople. The city on the Bosphorus, today's Istanbul, is the capital of the Ottoman Empire at this time. The Ottomans once ruled the most powerful empire in the world, but for years the empire has been in decline. It needs a big war – a big victory, ideally against the ambitious Russia – or it will perish. For this victory it needs a strong ally, and finds it in Germany.

"I see clearly enough now that Germany had made all her plans for world dominion and that the country to which I had been sent as American Ambassador was one of the foundation stones of the Kaiser's whole political and military structure. Had Germany not acquired control of Constantinople in the early days of the war, it is not unlikely that hostilities would have ended a few months after the Battle of the Marne. It was certainly an amazing fate that landed me in this great headquarters of intrigue at the very moment when the plans of the Kaiser for controlling Turkey, which he had carefully pursued for a quarter of a century, were about to achieve their final success."

Henry Morgenthau Senior, American ambassador to the Ottoman Empire from 1913 to 1918

Germany, September 1896. Wounded veterans of the Franco-Prussian War of 1871. The Battle of Sedan, won by the Germans on 1 September 1870, was crucial for victory in the Franco-Prussian War. Year after year the Germans celebrate Sedan Day on 2 September. Even decades later veterans of the war are revered as heroes, as in this photograph. In German propaganda the French are called the 'hereditary enemy'.

"When I was a child, you couldn't imagine a year without Sedan Day. After Sedan all that was left were parades. So when Ohm Krüger drove along Tauentzienstrasse after losing the Boer War in 1902, I was standing in line with my governess. Because it was unthinkable not to gaze in marvel at a gentleman in a top hat who reclined against the upholstered seat and had led a war, as they said. But to me it seemed magnificent and, at the same time, not quite well-mannered; as if the man had 'led' a rhinoceros or a dromedary and become famous that way. What could come after Sedan?"

Walter Benjamin, German philosopher

Hohenzieritz, Germany, before the war. The room where Queen Louise of Prussia, the great-great grandmother of German Emperor Wilhelm II, died. Louise was from the house of Mecklenburg-Strelitz, one of the oldest German princely families. Louise's aunt was the British monarch Queen Charlotte and her first cousin was the Crown Prince of Denmark. When Napoleon I defeated Prussia in 1806, Queen Louise saved the country with great diplomatic skill – and became an icon of Prussia.

"Sire, I know that you accuse me of getting involved in political matters. Sire, I am a wife and mother and as such I present to your heart the fate of Prussia – this country to which so many fetters bind me. I turn to your generous heart and plead and await joy from Your Majesty."

Louise von Mecklenburg-Strelitz, Queen of Prussia, to Napoleon (1776–1810)

▶ **Stettin Station, Berlin, Germany, before the war.** The beginning of the twentieth century was the birth of 'the mass': mass production, mass communication and mass transport. The railway is already a few decades old, but the automobile has only appeared in recent years. By the start of the First World War there are over 200 brands of automobile in Germany.

"The menace of Germany lies in her scientific organization. We are all agreed Prussian militarism must be crushed: so long as the world contains it, there is no safety in it for democracy. But what is Prussian militarism? It was not born yesterday: it was not born in 1914. It is an ancient sore. It is the bestial and inhuman expression of a philosophy, the outcome of a whole race so madly intoxicated with conceit that it imagines it is predestined to dominate the world, and is amazed to see free men dare to rise and contest its rights."

René Viviani, French minister, at the Waldorf Astoria, New York City, on 11 May 1917

Vatican, c. 1900. Pope Leo XIII in his private room. He is the pope who ushers the Catholic church into the modern technological era: the first pope to be filmed, the first whose voice is recorded.

"A few months before his death I was able to pay the pope my third and last visit. In spite of his great frailty, the 93-year-old came towards me and held out both hands. The pope said he had followed my style of government with interest, and been delighted to recognize that I constructed my rule on a firm basis of Christianity. It is guided by such high religious principles, he said, that he could do no other than to beg for a blessing for me, my dynasty and the German Reich, and give me his apostolic blessing. I was interested that on this occasion the pope said that Germany must become the sword of the Catholic church."

Wilhelm II, German Kaiser

Palestine, October 1898. Kaiser Wilhelm in the Holy Land. In 1869 Friedrich III, the father of Wilhelm II, bought the ruins of the Jerusalem Crusader church of St Maria Latina. Wilhelm II has the Lutheran Church of the Redeemer built on its site. On Reformation Day in 1898, Wilhelm II consecrates the church during his trip to Palestine.

"God has granted us the blessing of being able to consecrate the house of God erected in honour of the Redeemer of the World in this city sacred to all Christians, in a site consecrated by a real labour of love. What my forefathers have longed for more than half a century, and striven for, as sponsors and protectors of the labour of love founded here in the evangelical spirit, has found fulfilment through the building and consecration of the Church of the Redeemer."

Wilhelm II, in his address for the consecration of the Church of the Redeemer in Jerusalem

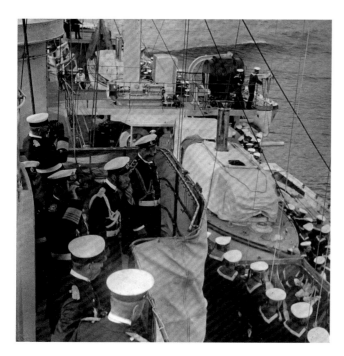

Kiel, Germany, before the war. Kaiser Wilhelm II and Tsar Nicholas II observe a joint German-Russian manoeuvre on board a German warship. The two rulers – third cousins – were close friends before the war. On the eve of the war Willy and Nicky, as they called each other, swapped a series of telegrams to avert the looming calamity.

Kilb, Austria-Hungary, before the war. The market community of Kilb in the Alpine foothills of Lower Austria. The written history of the area dates back to the time of the Romans, when it belongs to the province of Noricum. In the Middle Ages, Austria emerges as the Eastern Marches, or borderland, of the Holy Roman Empire, the then German state.

"Peterhof Palace, 29 July 1914
His Majesty the Emperor
New Palace
Am glad you are back. In this serious moment, I appeal to you to help me. An ignoble war has been declared to a weak country. The indignation in Russia shared fully by me is enormous. I foresee that very soon I shall be overwhelmed by the pressure forced upon me and be forced to take extreme measures which will lead to war. To try and avoid such a calamity as a European war I beg you in the name of our old friendship to do what you can to stop your allies from going too far.
Nicky"

Tsar Nicholas II

"In 1913 I went to the medical examination for the last time. Over the previous few years I had been lucky and walked free, as I had cut my thumb with a circular saw at the age of fifteen, and it had not healed properly. But this time I went to the examination apprehensively. Everything was fine, but when I was to make a fist, I couldn't because of my thumb. The doctor took my hand and tried, but again it didn't work. And he said to the other doctor, 'It's a real shame about this man. We can't take him, mark him as unfit.' And a weight fell from my heart."

Karl Kasser, Austrian farmer from Kilb

Schneidemühl, Germany, 1913. Elfriede Kuhr and her brother Willi-Gunther. They grow up in Schneidemühl, in the province of Posen, in their grandmother's house, as their mother is working in far-away Berlin. Elfriede starts keeping a diary on 1 August 1914.

"My name is Piete. I won't say my real name, it's too stupid. Or rather I will: Elfriede, Frieda. (Frieda is the worst!) My brother is called Willi-Gunther, he's fifteen years old. I'm twelve. We live with my grandmother in Schneidemühl, province of Posen. My mother has a music school in Berlin, the Master School for Stage and Concert. She visits us often. Those days are big celebrations."

Elfriede Kuhr, German schoolgirl

▶ **Berlin, Germany, before the war.** Traffic on Friedrichstrasse. The German Empire is the youngest of the major powers in Europe. Not founded until 18 January 1871, under the leadership of Prussia, it is still the economically strongest country in Europe. Along with Germany's rise in Europe, its capital, Berlin, enjoys a heyday.

"In fact I arrived in Berlin at a very interesting, historical moment. Since 1870, when Berlin had turned from the sober, small and far from wealthy capital of the kingdom of Prussia into the German Kaiser's city of residence, the unprepossessing town on the Spree had enjoyed a massive boom. But Berlin had not yet assumed leadership in artistic and cultural matters; Munich, with its painters and poets, was the actual centre of art, the Dresden Opera dominated music, and the small residences attracted valuable elements; above all, however, Vienna, with its centuries-old tradition, its concentrated power and its natural talent, had hitherto remained far superior to Berlin."

Stefan Zweig, Austrian writer

Berlin, Germany, 1913. At the beginning of the twentieth century Austria-Hungary, the huge and ancient double monarchy that had once ruled almost the whole of Europe, is only a colossus with feet of clay. The country consists of the Empire of Austria and the Kingdom of Hungary. But these, in turn, consist of a total of eight nations and seventeen countries – all of which are striving for more self-determination or independence.

"It was only with regard to art that everyone in Vienna felt an equal right, because in Vienna love and art were seen as a common duty, and the part that the Jewish bourgeoisie played in Viennese culture with help and patronage was huge. They were the actual audience, they filled the theatres, the concert-halls, they bought the books, the paintings, they visited the exhibitions and with their more agile intelligence, less burdened by tradition, they were always the sponsors and pioneers of everything new. Almost all of the great art collections of the nineteenth century were formed by them, almost all artistic experiments made possible by them; without the tireless stimulating interest of the Jewish bourgeoisie, thanks to the indolence of the court, the aristocracy and Christian millionaires, who preferred to keep riding stables and hunts rather than sponsor art, Vienna would have remained as far behind Berlin artistically as Austria was politically behind the German Reich."

Stefan Zweig, Austrian writer

Paris, France, 1896. French cavalry during the 'Tsar Days' – the days in which the Tsar was abroad on official state visits – in Paris. The war was supposed to begin like the wars of previous centuries: men in colourful uniforms whose purpose was to be seen, with flashing sabres and magnificent horses. But from the outbreak of war it becomes clearer by the day that with this war the age of technology, of machines, is beginning even on the battlefield.

Paris, France, 1896. The Tsar and Tsarina of Russia in Paris. The German Chancellor Otto von Bismarck's policy had always been the isolation of France in Europe. Thus in 1887 Germany, under Bismarck, had forged an alliance with Russia, to steal a march on France. But the new Kaiser, Wilhelm II, allowed this alliance to expire in 1890. Russia, now isolated, immediately looked around for a new ally, and in 1892 found it in France.

"Whence the aversion of a wide social strata for the cavalry? First of all it is the conceptual and deep-rooted opposition of the man who walks in dust against the rider who trots onwards apparently free of care and effort. Then the halo that has floated around horse and rider since ancient times may get on the nerves of some people who always see him as one of the last memories of the days when the craft of soldiery was still surrounded by glamour and lustre."

Hans von Seeckt, German general

"It is only Russia and France that make peace uncertain, and yappy Italy, which is always sticking its nose into everything."

Otto von Bismarck, German Chancellor

Tsar Nicholas II and Madame Fauré, the wife of the French President, in a carriage. President Fauré – also known as 'the Sun President' because of his extravagant lifestyle, in a reference to the Sun King Louis XIV – argued for an alliance between France and Russia all through his life.

"Diplomacy is the art of stroking the dog while the muzzle and leash aren't yet ready."

Felix Fauré

Tianjin, China, 1900.
The end of the nineteenth century sees a popular uprising in China against increasing foreign influence. The target of the so-called 'Boxers' – chiefly peasants who call themselves the fists of justice and harmony – are predominantly missionaries and Chinese Christians, who are killed in their hundreds. The Chinese government supports the Boxers and declares war on the major powers of Europe – Britain, France, Germany, Russia, Italy and Austria-Hungary – as well as Japan and the United States.

"The sun had risen when I opened my eyes in the morning. I forced myself to rise, washed my face, and asked for a little food, but could not get it down. Sitting down I heard loud talking and laughter among the guests. The topic of conversation was the massacre of foreigners the day before! One said: 'There were ten ocean men killed, three men, four women, and three little devils.' Then one after another added gruesome details, how the cruel swords had slashed, how the baggage had been stolen, how the very clothing had been stripped from the poor bodies, and how they had then been flung into a wayside pit."

Fei Ch'i-hao, Chinese Christian

◄ **Tianjin, China, 1900.** American artillery firing on Tientsin. The great powers are furious at the Chinese uprising, particularly over the massacre of Christian missionaries. When German troops are dispatched to China, Wilhelm II delivers his 'Hun speech'. It was on the basis of this that the Allies referred to the Germans as 'Huns' during the First World War.

"Just as a thousand years ago the Huns made a name for themselves which makes them seem powerful in tradition. May the name of Germany in China be confirmed in such a way that no Chinaman will ever dare to look askance at a German."

From Kaiser Wilhelm II's 'Hun speech'

Tianjin, China, 1900. French soldiers at their midday meal in the bullet-riddled station of Tientsin. China and the Boxers have no chance against the united force and modern weapons of the world's great powers. China loses the war, and has to accept a humiliating peace treaty in the form of the Boxer Protocol.

"At last our ears have heard the sweet music for which we have been listening for two months – the cannonading of the relief army – so plainly that we know that intense desire and imagination are not deceiving us, as so many times before. Our deliverance is at hand. Last night was a fearful one. There were at least six distinct attacks, the first beginning about eight in the evening, and there was almost incessant firing between these attacks. Our implacable foes seemed determined to use to the utmost this last chance to wipe us out. Our garrison returned fire more than at any other time, for now they are not afraid of exhausting their ammunition..."

Luella Miner, American professor in China

South Africa, 1900. A group of Boer leaders. 'Boer' is the term used to describe the descendants of Dutch colonists in the territory of present-day South Africa. Driven out of the British Cape colony, they found the Boer republics of the Orange Free State and the Transvaal. After large deposits of gold and diamonds are discovered there, war breaks out. Britain wants to annex the Boer republics, but the supposedly inferior Boers have bought the most modern weapons in France and Germany.

South Africa, 1900. Lord Roberts, British commander in the Boer War. In 1846 khaki uniforms had been introduced in the British Army, the first time that camouflage played a part in the choice of a uniform. After the Boer War, all the great powers carried out reforms in their uniforms. It is only in France that the characteristic red trousers are retained – until the First World War.

"The Boers seem to have started the hostilities, the whole of their reliance leaning on the strength and number of their cannons – and they are now surely discovering their mistake. I do not think that they will have more courage to do anything better than what they did on Wednesday and we can, therefore, expect that they will either go away or settle round us until they get further reinforcement."

Sol Plaatje, South African translator for the British troops during the Siege of Mafeking

"We remember well arriving at Paardeberg not long after Lord Roberts's famous march from Kimberley to Bloemfontein. The track of a great army is rather a curious thing to witness. Here is the field telegraph still standing, and there the deep marks of the wheels of gun carriages in the sand, and everywhere are carcasses of horses strewn in the way. Vultures fly low over the fields, or hop heavily across the sun-baked earth. Here and there are farm-houses, whose names have since become famous in history: 'Poplar's Grove', 'Driefontein'. Their walls are riddled with bullets, and in the garden, perhaps, shells are raked together into piles. In some quiet corner are the graves of those who have fallen, covered with heaps of stones."

Sarah Macnaughtan, Scottish nurse

South Africa, 1900. Military attachés of various states on the staff of Lord Roberts. As the Boers were able to import the latest weapons from Europe, the two armies with modern equipment face one another. This also brings the other great powers into play; they dispatch military attachés to study the war. The knowledge they share shapes the future strategies of the great powers, not least in the First World War.

"Boers are using some marvellous shells just now. Experts say that they are very new and must be made in Johannesburg. I wonder if the gunners who fire them appreciate the idea that they are better and deadlier than the brand 'Made in Germany'. They seldom burst when they first land, but merely plough through the ground for a little distance, then pump right up in the air again and start a fresh journey for one or two more miles before they reach their fag end."

Sol Plaatje, South African translator for the British troops during the Siege of Mafeking

"*The men who would do the Queen's business so well in Canada were not backward in coming forward to do her work in South Africa at the outbreak of the Boer War. To the first Canadian contingent which sailed in October 1899, the police were not called upon to contribute any officers or men, but some months later a second contingent was asked for, and the recruiting for this cause was placed in the hands of the Mounted Police.*"

Sarah Macnaughtan, Scottish nurse

Berlin, Germany, 24 May 1913. The imposing Berliner Stadtschloss, or Berlin Castle. On 24 May 1913 the daughter of Kaiser Wilhelm II marries Ernst-August of Hanover; the wedding is the last major event organized by the European aristocracy. King George V and Queen Mary travel to Berlin for the occasion, as does Tsar Nicholas II.

"*I cannot tell you how very much we enjoyed our visit to Berlin or how touched we were at the kindness shown us by William & Victoria & indeed by everybody. It was a most interesting time & so beautifully arranged in every way, nothing could have gone better.*"

Queen Mary, in a letter to her German great aunt

Berlin, Germany, 24 May 1913. Berlin sightseers at the wedding. Berlin's chief of police receives warnings that anarchists are mingling with the public in the city. There are thought to be twenty-five marksmen who want to assassinate the Tsar. If they are successful, it means war.

"The Berlin public greeted me much more warmly than my Russians. I am not used to such a warm, spontaneous welcome as I have had here."

Nicholas II, Tsar of Russia

▶ **Berlin, Germany, 24 May 1913.** A strong police presence like the one pictured thwarts any assassination attempt. After the wedding Tsar Nicholas II and King George V leave for home, while Kaiser Wilhelm II remains in Berlin. In just over a year he will be at war with his cousins.

"Victoria and I were so glad to have had you here and shall always remember the pleasant days we spent together."

Wilhelm II, in a telegram to Tsar Nicholas II

Constantinople, Ottoman Empire, 1917. During a visit from Kaiser Wilhelm II, His Majesty Sultan Mehmed V reviews the guard of honour. By the start of the twentieth century the once-mighty Ottoman Empire has lost much of its power. As there have been repeated wars against Russia in the Caucasus, the Empire has allied itself with Germany. One sign of this alliance is the construction of the Baghdad railway, which is to connect Berlin and Baghdad.

"*The station of Haidar Pasha is the biggest and most magnificent in Turkey – the architectural herald's cry of Anatolia's ascent to a new European life. All around, old cypresses mourn over silent Ottoman graves. On the pavement a noisy, chatty chaos of men wearing the tarbush, and czapkalis – hat-wearers – with women and children.* Hamals *(bearers) carry the luggage. Officers walk back and forth gossiping, just like lieutenants at home, except that they aren't flirting, at least not perceptibly, because such things do not exist for the devotees of the Prophet. The Turks travelling with us are noticeable from a distance, in that their women are really stowed away. They are emotional people; many of them travel first or second class, while their womenfolk have to cram themselves into the overcrowded* haremlik *of third-class goods, where they install themselves, squabbling and shouting, with their belongings. The train is rather long. Its corridor coaches are built on the model of our dining and sleeping cars, which gives the train as a whole an extremely feudal appearance. A few goods wagons are attached. One of them is full of recruits who were drafted in European Turkey, and who are now being transported to some garrison in Anatolia.*"

Adalbert Zimmermann, German traveller on the Baghdad railway

Port Arthur, Russia, 1904. Japanese cavalry on the battlefield in the Russo-Japanese War. In 1904 the first war of the twentieth century breaks out between the great powers of Russia and Japan. Three years previously, the two countries were allies in their joint invasion of China. The surprising defeat of Russia plunges the Tsar's empire into a deep crisis, while Japan becomes a great power once and for all.

"General Matsumura, one of the cleverest men in the Japanese Army, put himself at the head of the expedition and unfurled the banner of the Rising Sun which belonged to the Fourteenth Regiment. Barely fifteen minutes elapsed before the general leaped on shore and planted our country's flag in the square of Pitsevo, while a loud 'Banzai!' burst out like a peal of thunder. A detachment of Russians, seeing that resistance was futile, fired a few shots and retired hurriedly to the interior of the peninsula."

Hesibo Tikowara, Japanese sailor in the Russo-Japanese War

Russia, 1916. Tsar Nicholas II with his Cossack imperial guard. Nicholas II is effectively the last absolute ruler in Europe. Since the revolution of 1905 there has been a parliament, but power continues to rest with the Tsar – and with his advisers. Nicholas II is a weak ruler who is repeatedly led by the ministers and generals who advise him. The Tsar wishes at all cost to prevent a war with his cousin Wilhelm II, but preparations for war have been going on behind his back for a long time.

"The German Kaiser's love of peace guarantees that we ourselves will have to determine the moment of war."

Sergei Sazonov, Russian Foreign Minister, November 1913

Russia, 1914. Nicholas II's weakness – and the power of his advisers – are well known in Russia. His young son and successor Alexei also knows that only a strong ruler can save the Tsar's empire.

"When I am Tsar, no one will lie to me. I will bring order to this country."

Alexei, son of Tsar Nicholas II

▶ **Mexico, before the war.** Artillery exercise outside Mexico City. After a revolution breaks out in Mexico in 1910, there are repeated skirmishes with the United States along their common border. In 1914 the two countries sever diplomatic relations, after several American sailors are arrested on board their ship in the town of Tampico.

"It is my duty to call to your attention a situation which has arisen in our dealings with the General Victoriano Huerta at Mexico City which calls for action. On the ninth of April a paymaster of the USS Dolphin landed at the Iturbide Bridge landing at Tampico, and while engaged in loading the boat was arrested by an officer and squad of men of the army of General Huerta. The incident can not be regarded as a trivial one, especially as two of the men arrested were taken from the boat itself – that is to say, from the territory of the United States."

US President Woodrow Wilson, in his address to Congress, regarding the Tampico affair

Switzerland, 1912. Infantry on manoeuvre in Switzerland. In 1912 the Swiss army organized a major manoeuvre to which, amongst others, Kaiser Wilhelm II and observers from France and England are invited. The small Swiss army presents itself as extremely professional and well armed. This manoeuvre persuades strategists on both sides to respect Swiss neutrality during the war.

"Mobilization for war: the third of August is the first day of mobilization. All divisions, fortress crews, all Territorial Army units, all special troops. All communities bring horses and carts for appraisal in line with the horse stabling order."

Mobilization telegraph from the Swiss parliament, 31 July 1914

Romania, before the war.
A castle in Romania. In 1866 the Romanian parliament elects Carol I of the house of Hohenzollern, from which Kaiser Wilhelm is also descended, as the country's ruler. At this time Romania is still formally a part of the Ottoman Empire, and becomes independent only in 1877. Carol I brings the young country into an alliance with his relative Wilhelm II. But his successor Ferdinand is influenced by his wife, Marie of Edinburgh, who argues for an alliance with Britain.

"I look back and see visions of my country as for twenty-three years I have known it, peaceful, blooming, full of abundance, its vast plain an ocean of waving corn amongst which diligent peasants move to and fro gathering in the harvest, the land's dearest pride. I see its humble villages hidden amongst fruit trees, I see the autumn splendour of its forests, I see the grand solitude of its mountain summits, I see its noble convents, corners of hidden beauty, treasures of ancient art, I hear the sound of the shepherd's horn, the sweet complaint of his ditties."

Queen Marie of Romania

Romania, before the war. A peasant family in Romania. Before independence in 1877 Romania – like the rest of the Balkans – had been for centuries part of the Ottoman Empire. Only Transylvania, the majority of whose population is also Romanian, belongs to Austria-Hungary.

"The conquest and disappearance of that presence embedded in the living flesh of Europe of an alien substance – the Ottoman Turk – has permitted these countries, Romania, Serbia, Greece, Bulgaria, to escape from the Turkish whirlpool that for centuries had sucked them under."

Winifred Gordon, British author

Paris, France, before the war. In Paris in the summer of 1914 there is as yet no sense of the impending world war. The big story in the papers is the trial of Henriette Caillaux, the wealthy wife of the Finance Minister. On 16 March 1914 she shot the newspaper editor Gaston Calmette for leading a smear campaign against her husband. Her lawyer defends her by saying that, in a state of acute mental distress, she was unable to control her overwhelming female emotions. She is acquitted – on 28 June 1914, the same day on which Archduke Franz Ferdinand of Austria-Hungary is murdered.

"*I had expressed willingness to remain at my post in Paris until the early autumn, inasmuch as 'a quiet summer was expected'. Spring was a busy time for newspapermen. There had been the sensational assassination of Gaston Calmette, editor of the* Figaro, *by Mme Caillaux, wife of the cabinet minister. Then there was the 'caving-in' of the streets of Paris, owing to the effect of storms on the thin surface left by the underground tunnelling for the electric tramways, and for the new metropolitan 'tubes'. The big prize fight between Jack Johnson and Frank Moran for the heavyweight championship of the world followed. Finally, the day of the 'Grand Prix de Paris' brought the news of the murder at Sarajevo of the heir to the Austro-Hungarian throne.*"

Charles Inman Barnard, Paris correspondent of the *New York Tribune*

◄ **Paris, France, before the war.**
The promenade along the Seine in Paris. After losing the Franco-Prussian war of 1870–71 France becomes a republic – under the sceptical eye of the surrounding monarchs. The ensuing belle epoque was a time of peace, of travel, globalization, art, pleasure and technology – until July 1914. Within a few days a local conflict between Austria-Hungary and Serbia had become a world war.

"One beautiful afternoon toward the end of June 1914, I stopped at the gate of Jacques Blanche's house at Auteuil. It was a perfect summer day. Outside in the quiet street stood a long line of motors, and on the lawn and about the tea-tables there was a happy stir of talk. An exceptionally gay season was drawing to its close, the air was full of new literary and artistic emotions, and that dust of ideas with which the atmosphere of Paris is always laden sparkled like motes in the sun. I joined a party at one of the tables, and as we sat there a cloud-shadow swept over us, abruptly darkening bright flowers and bright dresses. 'Haven't you heard? The Archduke Ferdinand assassinated ... at Sarajevo ... where is Sarajevo? His wife was with him. What was her name? Both shot dead.'"

Edith Wharton, American novelist living in France

Berlin, Germany, before the war. The streets of Berlin. The murder of the successor to the Austrian throne marks the beginning of the 'July crisis', during which the countries of Europe manoeuvre their way into what is soon an unavoidable war. At the same time, many men volunteer for the army.

"I wept as I wrote my will. It was a detailed and formally correct document in which I appointed Aunt Michel, with whom I live, the sole inheritor of my visible and invisible estate as well as my debts. Should Aunt Selma no longer be alive, my parents were to assume charge of this inheritance. I then spoke volubly about my attitude to death and my previous colourful life, indicated how often I had been hungry and had nowhere to live, and what lovely plans I had had. I explained that I was aware that I had done many bad things and asked all those concerned and God to forgive me."

Joachim Ringelnatz, German sailor and author

Milan, Italy, before the war. Before the First World War Italy was in the Triple Alliance with Germany and Austria-Hungary. This alliance was to serve as a counterweight to the Triple Entente between France, England and Russia. But for Italy, the Triple Alliance is an alliance of convenience – and for many Italians Austria-Hungary is more of an enemy than an ally.

"I remained in silence for a while. We were propped on the sill of the large window: the summer morning drew a solemn and majestic purity from the thick greenery of the public gardens. The gardens were filled with children playing. A war? The war? An immense war? 'Small colonial wars will still take place,' said another man, 'but European wars are a nonsense, an anachronism, especially due to the concrete, unquestionable, self-evident fact, as the lawyers say, that there is greater respect for human life! But there's something else: governments of a kind that are still feudal, they have to think twice! The Internationale *today is a power, especially in Germany. In any event the Kaiser, for all his rather medieval fancy dress, is an amiable man, an honest, peaceable, travelling salesman of articles made in Germany."*

Alfredo Panzini, Italian author

Berlin, Germany, before the war. The Brandenburg Gate was erected to commemorate the victory of the Prussian King Frederick the Great in the Seven Years War against Austria (1756–1763). Until the abdication of the Kaiser in 1918, only two families were allowed to use the middle thoroughfare of the gate: the Kaiser's family and the von Pfuels. The Kaiser granted this honour to the family in gratitude to Ernst von Pfuel, commander of the Prussian sector of Paris in 1815, who had overseen the return of the Quadriga – taken by Napoleon to Paris – to the top of the gate.

"All of our Kaiser's work was devoted to the preservation of peace. If all his efforts should prove in vain, if we are forced to take up our swords again, we will go into the field with a good conscience and the knowledge that it was not we who wanted war. We will then fight the battle for our existence and our national honour to the very last drop of blood. In the gravity of this hour I would remind you of the words that Prince Friedrich Karl once called to the people of Brandenburg: 'Let your hearts beat for God and your fists strike the foe'."

Reich Chancellor Bethmann-Hollweg in a speech to the people of Berlin on 31 July 1914

El Paso, Texas, USA, before the war. A funeral in El Paso. From 1823 onwards, US foreign policy is defined by the Monroe Doctrine, which states that the US is to stay out of conflicts in Europe as long as the countries of Europe stay out of conflicts in America. With the start of the First World War this neutrality is put sorely to the test, as most newspapers hold Germany responsible for the war.

"Does the war fever make the whole world delirious? Are all feelings and emotions suddenly reversed, the sympathies of yesterday nothing but hatred today? Is the gigantic tragedy of Europe to be accompanied by a travesty of war on the pages of the American paper world? We live in a neutral country. Washington is not Petersburg; and yet can the outbursts of enmity toward Germany be harsher in the Tsar's country than on Broadway?"

Hugo Münsterberg, German-American psychologist

Texas, USA, before the war. In spite of the widespread anti-German mood in the USA, life continues as normal – as at this bullfight in Texas. From the start of the war President Wilson not only defends the neutrality of his country, he sends peace missions to the belligerent states. At the same time many volunteers – both men and women – travel from America to Europe and thus into the war.

"When the great war broke out, I was mildly sympathetic with England, and mighty sorry in an indefinite way for France and Belgium; but my sympathies were not strong enough in any direction to get me into uniform with a chance of being killed. Nor, at first, was I able to work up any compelling hate for Germany. The abstract idea of democracy did not figure in my calculations at all."

R. Derby Holmes, American volunteer in the British Army

Paris, France, 1896. The last major war in Europe – the Franco-Prussian War of 1870–71 – was decided by, among other things, the German troops being able to mobilize faster than expected because of the country's superior rail network. With the outbreak of war in 1914, trains containing hundreds of thousands of young soldiers now criss-cross the countries of Europe again.

"Six am, 4 September, in a moving train.
Here I am, forty hours on a journey whose picturesqueness outbalances its extreme discomforts. The great trouble is to get any sleep, and the problem is not easily solved when you are forty men penned up in a single cattle car. At every moment the train stops to make way for trains filled with the unfortunate civil population who are being removed from the war zone. Then come the trains carrying the wounded, a fine patriotic spectacle; then those with the English army, the artillery, etc. We know nothing about what is going on, as we no longer have any newspapers and we cannot put any dependence on the rumours which circulate among the terror-stricken inhabitants of the towns we pass through. Splendid weather."

Anonymous French soldier

THE BEGINNING

"My God, what does it all mean? Are men so mad? And why are they killing all our best and bravest?
Now the sons of my friends are falling fast – Duncan Sim's boy,
young Wilson, Neville Strutt, and scores of others."

Sarah Macnaughtan, Scottish nurse

On the evening of 1 August 1914, the German ambassador in St Petersburg, Count Friedrich Pourtalès, handed over the German declaration of war to the Russian foreign ministry. 'This is a criminal act, and the curse of the nations will befall you,' Russia's foreign minister Sergei Sazonov told him. 'We are only defending our honour,' responded Count Pourtalès. But Sazonov did not let him finish: 'It wasn't about your honour. One word would have been enough to maintain peace.' And yet Sazonov was one of those on the Russian side who had been trying to bring about a war for years.

Five weeks had now passed since the murder of the Austrian hier to the throne, Franz Ferdinand. They were weeks characterized by a flurry of diplomatic activity, partly to prevent war, partly to prevent peace. Not even the international public doubted the involvement of Serbian higher military circles in the machinations of Bosnian nationalist groups and

At the start of the war, these Austro-Hungarian soldiers sing as they go into battle in decorated railway carriages. No one sings on the way back in the wounded troop transports.

their assassination of the heir to the throne. Consequently, the Serbian government strove to comply with Austria's demands for an explanation. It was only when Austria-Hungary issued its ultimatum that Serbia accept constraints to its sovereignty that the mood in Europe turned. When Austria-Hungary declared war on Serbia on 28 July, the two central powers were already seen as the real warmongers by the rest of Europe.

At the eleventh hour, Britain's ruling powers attempted to avert the catastrophe. King George V sent an imploring telegram to Tsar Nicholas: 'I can only believe that a misunderstanding has led to this impasse. I am incredibly concerned that the opportunity to avoid this terrible fate, a fate that now threatens the whole world, could be left untaken.' With the help of this royal initiative, Foreign Minister Sir Edward Grey hoped to be able to maintain the opportunity for negotiations. 'If even just a brief pause could be won,' he wrote to the British ambassador in Berlin on 1 August, 'we could perhaps still keep the peace.'

But it was already too late. The German ambassador in St Petersburg was shocked when the Russian troops received the order to attack. By the evening of 1 August 1914, they were already marching towards East Prussia.

Austro-Hungarian soldiers keep watch from a church tower. Because they provide a panoramic view, church towers are popular artillery targets.

The following day was a Sunday. People all over Europe had time to come out of their houses on this sunny day and experience the outbreak of the war together. In his autobiography, Stefan Zweig recalls encountering 'something grand, captivating and even seductive' in Vienna as war broke out: 'Every single person experienced an enhancement of the self; he was no longer the isolated individual of yesterday, but part of a mass, he was of the people, and his person, his previously unnoticed person, had taken on new meaning.' The German philosopher and Nobel Prize Laureate Rudolf Eucken declared the war to be a 'source of moral strengthening'. The theologian and author Gustav Frenssen was convinced that God himself was at work in the 'Holy Battle' of the German people. Historian Friedrich Meinecke declared the outbreak of war to be 'one of the most wonderful moments of his life'.

Austro-Hungarian soldiers put up wire obstacles. Barbed wire was originally developed to protect grazing livestock.

(*Opposite*) The German Kaiserin and the Archduke of Hessen. Kaiser Wilhelm II is a close relative of the British King and the Russian Tsar.

Enthusiasm was riding high on the Place de le Concorde in Paris, too, where a cavalry regiment had been gathered. The artist Paul Maze reported that the officers looked very elegant in their white gloves, and that they were cheered on by an excited crowd with cries of 'à Berlin!' Infantry and artillery passed through the city en route to the train stations. The cannons in particular garnered a great deal of attention as they were decorated with flower garlands. Inspired by the enthusiasm, the officials of the French Ministry of War appealed to the leader of the Russian military mission, Count Ignatiev, to advance Russian troops to Berlin. That was an interesting suggestion, commented Russian tactician General Nikolai Golovin: tantamount to advising someone to commit suicide.

But the mood wasn't as euphoric everywhere as the pictures of 1 and 2 August implied. Young academics and artists in the capital cities were not swept up by the enthusiasm for long, as military historian Jeffrey Verhey discovered. They supplied photo opportunities for photographers and provided historians with quotations. In Berlin, one eyewitness commented on the 'women with tear-stained faces' not depicted in the newspapers. In the working-class district of Moabit in Berlin, a pastor wrote: 'Poverty is taking its toll on people,' and around him he saw none of the 'academic excitement that only the educated classes can afford, not needing to worry about where their next meal is coming from'. The records of the Bavarian parish Osterbuch bei Dillingen reported this of the Sunday service: 'The men were crying, the women sobbing'. And in Ebingen, in the Swabian Alps: 'our souls are filled with horror'.

The majority of socialists of almost all the states involved were convinced that the war in Europe was about defence and self-preservation. Most of the Social Democrat members of the Reichstag voted in favour of war credits.

In Germany, the unanimity of support for the war was referred to as the 'August Experience'. The Kaiser no longer recognized individual parties and declared a party truce. In France, socialists voted in favour of President Raymond Poincaré's *'Union sacrée'* and, in August, joined the government of Prime Minister René Viviani. The reformist socialist Jean Jaurès, together with Aristide Briand (joint founders of the workers' paper *l'Humanité*) championed peace with great public impact before deciding to support the defence of France shortly before the outbreak of war. Jaurès was subsequently murdered by a French nationalist. At his burial on 4 August, one day after Germany had declared war on

France, Léon Jouhaux, chairman of the syndicate union CGT, proclaimed that: 'We never wanted this war'. But, he added, that it now had to be waged nonetheless. 'We will be soldiers of peace in order to achieve peace for the Empire, in order to establish harmony between the peoples and the free partnership of nations.' The leader of the British Labour Party, Ramsay MacDonald, opposed Britain entering the war but was outvoted in the House of Commons. He subsequently stepped down as party leader. His successor, Arthur Henderson, joined the coalition cabinet of Liberal Prime Minister Herbert Henry Asquith in 1915.

In St Petersburg, which was renamed Petrograd when war broke out, the Social Democrats were not asking themselves whether they should become part of a government of the autocratic Tsarist regime. The mood here, and in other Russian cities, was particularly evident in the anti-German demonstrations taking place. The climax of this was

Austro-Hungarian soldiers receive their wages.

(*Opposite*) An Austro-Hungarian sentry with guard dog at the Dolomite front. Millions of dogs are used by all sides during the war.

the storming and plundering of the German embassy building. Designed by Peter Behrens, it had been completed and inaugurated only the previous year. But even this did not mean the desire for war was widespread. While British military attaché Colonel Knox did admittedly observe groups of young men cheering on the streets, he was much more moved by the women sobbing quietly, and the many serious and sombre-looking men.

In the small towns and large cities of France, Austria-Hungary and Germany, soldiers were waved off at the train stations by mayors and dignitaries, all hoping that 'By Christmas we will be back home again'.

For August Fuhrmann, the outbreak of war meant that he was forced to drastically change the focus of his work. Travel around the world was no longer possible, and so his photographs of far-flung places were replaced with images of war – a new field with which he could captivate his audience.

Postcard, Germany, 1914. German Kaiser Wilhelm II and Emperor Franz Joseph I of Austria-Hungary. As recently as 1866, Wilhelm's grandfather Wilhelm I and Emperor Franz Joseph had waged a fierce war against one another. Now Germany is the only ally of the collapsing Austro-Hungarian monarchy. On 28 July 1914, Austria-Hungary declares war on Serbia.

"It was the first time that the German-Austrian alliance was to demonstrate its strength and resilience before a serious conflict. In my Reichstag speeches, as in my instructions to our representatives abroad, I left no doubt that Germany was determined to maintain the alliance with Austria-Hungary with Nibelung loyalty. The German sword had been thrown into the scales of European decision-making, directly for our Austro-Hungarian ally, indirectly for the preservation of European peace and primarily for Germany's reputation and position in the world."

Bernhard Fürst von Bülow, German Chancellor

▶ **Germany, before the war.** Kaiser Wilhelm II with his soldiers. Three days after Austria-Hungary's declaration of war on Serbia, the Kaiser announces a state of war in Germany. War is declared against Russia a day later. Within a week, the local conflict has become a world war.

"We, Wilhelm, by God's grace Emperor of Germany and King of Prussia, decree on the basis of Article 68 of the constitution of the German Reich the following: The territory of the Reich, excluding the territorial parts of the Kingdom of Bavaria, is declared to be in a state of war. This order is valid from the day of its release.

Authenticated by our personal signature and the Imperial seal."

Wilhelm II

Berlin, Germany, early August 1914. People in Berlin cheer the declaration of war. The German Empire was united in three victorious nineteenth-century wars – against Denmark (1864), Austria (1866) and France (1870–71). In 1914, the Germans expect another quick victory.

"A German, who was resident in France before the war and crossed the border in August 1914, described to me the attitude towards the war on either side of the Rhine. 'You remember,' he said, 'those curiously hot, oppressively sultry July days. The air was heavy, dust whirled up all over the place, but the redemptive storm did not come. It was as if it was holding its breath. Then there was a rumble. A mute cry ran through France. No one could believe it.' And then the storyteller crossed the Rhine. 'My mind froze. I thought I had come to a country fair. Bells ringing, garlands, free beer, cheers and shouts – my homeland was one big fairground, and they hadn't the faintest idea of the war they were about to enter.'"

Kurt Tucholsky, German writer

Germany, 1900. Central Europe has enjoyed forty-three years of peace. The fighting has gone on elsewhere – in the Balkans, in South Africa and Asia – but people have forgotten the horrors of war, and propaganda gives them only the image of heroic struggle. The war begins with what will later be known in Germany as the 'August experience' – millions of young men want to go into battle, they just don't want to arrive too late. Nothing would be worse than to miss the long-awaited, glorious victory.

"A swift excursion into romanticism, a wild and manly adventure – that was how the war was painted in 1914 in the mind of the simple man, and young people were even honestly worried that they might miss some marvellous excitement in their lives; so they rallied impetuously around the flags, so they cheered and sang in the processions that brought them to the slaughter, and the red wave of blood flowed feverishly through the veins of the whole Reich."

Stefan Zweig, Austrian writer

Vienna, Austria-Hungary, before the war. In marvellous parades like this one in Vienna in the summer of 1914, millions of young men go off to a war that so many of them will not survive. By October of that year there has already been a second wave of recruitment in Austria-Hungary to replace the many soldiers who fell in the first months of the war.

"They now enlisted men up to the age of forty-two, the misery was endless. The ones already in the field were soldiers heart and soul. They were always successful, too. It continued like that for a while, but then things went backwards. Weeks passed like that, and whole regiments needed to be replaced. Men who had previously been unfit were called up. Even I was considered fit. Even though I couldn't help reflecting that there were so many people who had to join in, my heart was heavy when I thought of having to abandon all things dear to me, and go off into the unknown. On 15 January 1915, in severe cold, we had to set off."

Karl Kasser, Austrian soldier

Russian Poland, c. 1914. The enthusiastic soldiers are soon followed by a second wave. Millions of women want to make their contribution to the expected victory. They volunteer for service, as Red Cross nurses like those pictured here. Very few have medical training, and none can imagine the horror that awaits them.

"We, for our part, were 'military', and bandaged little messenger boys with the rest. We talked about 'rashions' and 'revellies', and marched (rather badly, I am afraid) through London, but the Sunday crowds cheered us, and I do believe we all felt like doing our bit. The messenger boys' wounds were always conveniently placed, and they never screamed and writhed or prayed for morphia when they were being bandaged."

Sarah Macnaughtan, volunteer nurse from Scotland

Berlin, Germany, 2 September 1896. The Brandenburg Gate in Berlin decorated for Sedan Day, when Germany celebrates its victory over France in 1870. For the French, Sedan was a national trauma. 'Never speak of it, always think of it,' they say about the Battle of Sedan.

"*Monday, 10 August. Ninth day of mobilization. Hot, sunny weather. Temperature at 5pm 29 degrees centigrade. Light southerly breeze. Depicted on all faces this morning is anxious but confident expectation, for the public are conscious that a desperate encounter between two millions of men is impending in Belgium and on the Alsace-Lorraine border from Liège to Colmar. I met today M. Hedeman, the correspondent of the* Matin, *who recently witnessed the arrival of Emperor William and the Crown Prince in Berlin, which he compared to the departure of Napoleon III for Sedan in 1870.*"

Charles Inman Barnard, Paris correspondent of the *New York Tribune*

Postcard, Germany, beginning of the war. Propaganda begins immediately after the outbreak of war. In German schools, pupils are taught not to use words from the languages of the enemy countries.

"*In school the teachers say we have a duty to the fatherland to stop using foreign words. At first I didn't know what they meant. Now I get it: from now on we're not allowed to say 'Adieu' because it's French. It's an honour to say 'Lebewohl' or 'Auf Wiedersehen', or perhaps 'Grüss Gott'. From now on I have to call Mama 'Mutter', but 'Mutter' isn't affectionate enough. I want to say 'Muttchen'.*"

Elfriede Kuhr, German schoolgirl

VENDANGES en BOURGOGNE « A la Grande Châtelaine »   Ronco aîné, édit. - Beaune (Déposé)

Burgundy, France, before the war. The harvest in Burgundy. The saying 'An army marches on its stomach' is attributed to Napoleon I, and to coincide with mobilization, grain and cattle are requisitioned across France to feed the armies at the front. Initially this leads to food shortages. Things don't improve later, as food producers have to make up for the loss of men sent to the front.

"Along with emergency mobilization, the Army Ministry acted to requisition foodstuffs, and now Parisians began vying to lay in supplies of vegetables and other groceries. Hearing about this made me realize that such things could not simply be attributed to the individualism of Europeans. Rather, I came to appreciate the dreadful effects of economic panic. I could no longer listen indifferently to stories about people killing cats and mice for food during the Franco-Prussian War. And even now I recall a passage in Tayama Katai's eyewitness account from the Russo-Japanese War of battlefield correspondents fighting over rice balls. It frightened me to think that, if the day ever came when we were confined to the Japanese embassy, we too might find ourselves fighting over a rice ball."

Tōson Shimazaki, Japanese author in Paris

▶ **Russian Poland, c. 1914.** The war should have been won by Christmas 1914 – or so the generals thought in Germany, France, England, Austria and Russia. In fact, by Christmas all military strategies have failed. Millions of soldiers live in the trenches and have to prepare for a long war. The provision of supplies for them in the field, which was inadequately planned for at the beginning of the war, now has top priority. And it is not only a matter of ammunition, food and clothing – for the first time the soldiers are granted cigarette rations. Some of the cigarettes are rolled by women volunteers, like those ones shown here.

"In October we had weekly collections of cigars, cigarettes and tobacco, and by 1 March these had produced about 16,000 cigars, 3,000 cigarettes and 450 packs of tobacco. Three hundred one-pound dispatch-ready parcels of charitable donations from school pupils were delivered, and two big collections of charitable donations organized before Christmas, provided by Ersatz battalions and collection points."

Thirty-seventh annual report of the Leibniz School in Hanover, 1915

Russian Poland, c. 1914. Without the men who have gone into the field of battle, the women left at home have to look after their children on their own. And even worse – millions of children will grow up without their fathers, who will never return from this war.

"My God, what does it all mean? Are men so mad? And why are they killing all our best and bravest? Now the sons of my friends are falling fast – Duncan Sim's boy, young Wilson, Neville Strutt, and scores of others. I know one case in which four brothers have fallen; another, where twins of nineteen died side by side; and this one has his eyes blown out, and that one has his leg torn off, and another goes mad; and boys, creeping back to the base holding an arm on, or bewildered by a bullet through the brain, wander out of their way till a piece of shrapnel or torn edge of shell finds them, and they fall again, with their poor boyish faces buried in the mud!"

Sarah Macnaughtan, Scottish nurse

Western front, France, c. 1915. A French parade of troops. In France, too, many soldiers go into war with great expectations. Apart from making amends for the defeat at Sedan, the reconquest of Alsace-Lorraine is France's chief military goal. The whole strategy of the French military leadership is aimed at a quick and overwhelming victory.

Russian Poland, c. 1914. German Uhlans riding through Russian Poland. Russia begins the war with a major offensive into German East Prussia. Most of the German armies are deployed against France, but the Russian advance is halted in the battles of Tannenberg and the Masurian lakes. Losses are so great that the general of the Russian 2nd Army commits suicide rather than admit defeat to his Tsar.

"Ah! Such pangs in my heart. Having arrived here, we were parted, André going to Hédouville barracks and I to the law courts. There were four of us, and how hard it was for us, particularly for the first night, to sleep under the stars. We rang on everyone's doors. But everywhere was full, or else they didn't reply. In the end we rang so much that a door opened: it was the presbytery. So that was where I spent my first night, on a bale of straw. We managed two hours of good sleep. I thought of you, my dear one, sure that if you knew you would be happy; let us hope that this protection will not abandon me, and that it is a good omen. Ah! My dear Suzanne, such pangs in my heart, if we turn back, if we think of all the ones who stayed back there, whom we love so much."

Alexandre Jacqueau, French soldier

"The Russians, with their sanguine temperament, hoped for a permanent local success. They forgot the alternate marsh and sand of Northern Poland, which had been purposely left without railways and roads to delay an enemy's advance. They forgot the wonderful capacity of the East Prussian railway system. They sent the 2nd Army forward without field bakeries, imagining, if they thought of the soldiers' stomachs at all, that a large army could be fed in a region devoid of surplus supplies. They probably imagined that during the strain of the campaign in Western Europe the enemy's opposition would be less serious than it actually proved. They took no count of the inferiority of the Russian machine to the German in command and armament and in power of manoeuvre."

Major General Alfred Knox, British liaison officer in Russia

Austria-Hungary, 1914. Austrian soldier Karl Kasser. While Russia suffers two serious defeats in East Prussia, the Russian troops who march at the same time into Austria-Hungary do significantly better. In the battle in Galicia they inflict almost half a million losses on the Austrian armies in two weeks. To prevent a total collapse of the front, new regiments are quickly raised in Austria.

"On the 17th we went to confession and communion. There was no leave in this regiment. So on the 18th, without seeing our loved ones, we had to go to the front. A parcel of food and money, which I urgently needed, reached me at the very last moment. That was a real pleasure. We marched down crowded streets to the station amidst much singing and music. With our rifles and our collars garlanded with flowers, cheered on by the shouts of our compatriots, we headed towards our doom."

Karl Kasser, Austrian soldier

▶ **Russian Poland, c. 1914.** Poland was once one of the biggest and most powerful countries in Europe – until Prussia, Russia and Austria divide it between them. In the First World War confrontation between Germany – to which Prussia belongs – and Austria on the one hand, and Russia on the other, Poles fight against Poles for the warring powers. Many of the war's bloodiest battles are fought on territory which was part of the former Poland.

"My husband was not in the country with us, but in Suwalki for a few days, and I wondered why he did not come on the evening of the first of August. We waited dinner, and were sure he would be there, as he is a man who never disappoints. After being most wakeful, I fell, towards morning, into a very sound sleep, only to be awakened about four o'clock by a violent rapping on my window. I sprang up quickly in order to still the noise before the children should be aroused, thinking something was needed by the servant going into the town to the market. There I was confronted by Fate in the form of my husband's man, Jan, white and solemn-faced. 'My lady, there is war,' and he handed me a card from my husband."

Laura de Gozdawa Turczynowicz, an American woman living in Russian Poland, married to a Polish nobleman

"*Friedman has innumerable good war jokes, but they all lose so in the translation. 'Why does the old Austrian Emperor always carry his head so bowed now?' 'He is looking for Belgrade – which the army laid at his feet last year.'*

Or 'Do you know the new Viennese dance for the Carnival?' 'No, what is it like?' 'It is called Potiorek (the Austrian General) – it is quite original – two steps forwards and six steps backwards!'"

Ethel Cooper, Australian piano teacher in Leipzig

Western front, Belgium, c. 1915. Before the First World War only the United Kingdom had a professional army of voluntarily serving soldiers. For that reason the British Army is much smaller than those of the Continental powers of France, Germany, Russia and Austria – but on the other hand, it is highly professional. In autumn 1914 all the armies have to train many new recruits as quickly as possible. Accidents are a regular occurrence.

"This is written with three fingers of my left hand, which have now been set free. I am going on splendidly. The surgeon says I shall be on parade in a fortnight, and my burns pain very little now. I was in the middle of a group of thirty men, instructing them, and there was a bag of twelve pounds of gunpowder in front of my right foot. Some spark must have reached it. There was not a great report, but a strong flame. The five of us who were nearest had our uniforms charred black, and all the exposed skin of hands and faces more or less burnt. One sergeant, Day, was stooping and caught it in the eyes, but they are sure that he is not blind."

Sergeant C.E. Montague, in a letter to his wife

Romagné, France, c. 1915. The longer the war lasts, the more important the military postal service becomes for the soldiers. Many of them first learn to read and write in the trenches. In the conquered territories, as here, outside a post office in Romagné, the service is soon connected to the national postal service. Letters in both directions are strictly censored as the military authorities are afraid that soldiers might inadvertently give away battle plans or troop movements. It is also important that those who remain at home must not know how serious things really are in the trenches. The general public often know only the reports from the newspapers – and these write only about victories.

"Dear Frau R.!
Recently I have been in the doldrums, because
for weeks I have heard little or nothing from
everybody, including you. Perhaps the field post is
partly responsible for that, because as we hear, all
kinds of delays are supposed to be occurring.
*   I received your little box of chocolate and*
apple purée. Things like that make a nice snack
on night duty, an aid against tiredness."

Gerrit Engelke, German soldier, in a letter

RED CROSS NURSES & DOCTORS FROM JAPAN GOING TO EUROPE

Japan, 1915. Japanese nurses and doctors on their way to Europe. When war breaks out in Europe, Japan makes an offer to England to join the war on the side of the Entente – if, in return, it is allowed to occupy German colonies in eastern Asia, particularly the fortress of Tsingtao. On 23 August 1914, Japan declares war on Germany.

"As with our relations with America, our relationship with Japan passed through a period of bad blood. Until the early Nineties, we had served as a model for the Japanese, and been considered a friend, and the Japanese proudly called themselves the Prussia of the East."

Bernhard von Bülow, German Chancellor

Russian Poland, c. 1915. German soldiers by a monument near a Polish farmhouse. After its victories at Tannenberg and the Masurian lakes, the German army invades Russian Poland.

"The first soldier was soon followed by his comrades. Then an officer, who rounded the corner, coming to a stop directly before our windows. An old Jewess stepped out and saying, 'Guten Tag,' handed him a packet of papers, and gave various directions with much gesticulation. A spy at our very door! A woman I had seen many times! Busy with Wladek I saw no more for a while when a cry from the two other children made me rush to the window. They were coming into our court. The soldiers! And in a moment rushed into the room where we were, in spite of the signs tacked up on all doors 'Tyfus'. Seeing me in the Red Cross uniform they held back a moment. One bolder than his comrades laughed saying, 'She is trying to deceive us,' and came toward me with a threatening gesture. Then with all my fear, God gave me strength to defy them. In German, which fortunately I speak very well, I asked what they wanted."

Laura de Gozdawa Turczynowicz, an American woman living in Russian Poland

Kutno, Russian Poland, c. 1915. Market traffic in the small Polish town of Kutno. The German advance into Russian Poland soon grinds to a standstill. The territory is the same as that which led to the Russian defeats in East Prussia; there are hardly any railways and only a few paved roads, which makes troop movements and the supply of provisions very difficult.

"Then we soon reached the final destination of our journey. The last stop, Ruszgolyana, was a larger village, but one with nothing to show but little huts and cottages covered with shingles. In the village street, which we had to pass along, there was indescribable dirt up to our ankles. As a result our new uniforms were soon splashed with filth. Worst of all, our boots and ankle gaiters were pulled off, inches thick with dirt. The cause lay in the unfamiliar excess of military vehicles using the road, the rain had finally also done its part. Also the road was neither paved nor in any other way made fit for heavy vehicles."

Alfred Lempelius, German soldier

◀ **Janów, Russian Poland, c. 1915.**
German troops pose for a picture by Polish windmills. News trickles slowly through to the soldiers that the war is not going as planned. Even among the German troops in Russian Poland, whose campaign is the most successful of all, no end to the war is in sight. It is even worse for the new French recruits on the western front, who are not informed about the huge losses that they have to replace.

"We learn from wounded refugees that in the first days of August mistakes were made in the high command which had terrible consequences. It falls to us now to repair those mistakes.

Well, this war will not have been the mere march-past which many thought, but which I never thought it would be; but it will have stirred the good in all humanity. I do not speak of the magnificent things which have no immediate connection with the war – but nothing will be lost."

Anonymous French soldier

Constantinople, Ottoman Empire, 1917. Kaiser Wilhelm II, Sultan Mehmed V and Enver Pasha board a coach. Unlike Germany, which is accustomed to victory, the Ottoman Empire lost its last major conflict against Russia (1877–78). The Empire forges an alliance with Germany, declaring war on the Entente in order to win back the territories it lost at that time. Winston Churchill, the First Lord of the Admiralty, suggests attacking the Ottoman capital, Constantinople, with warships. In order to do so, the Gallipoli Peninsula must first be conquered.

"An observation balloon looked up over the western horizon, there was a sudden thunder, and all at once the sky above Gallipoli rained screaming shells and death. You can imagine how that hurricane of fire, sweeping in without warning, from people knew not where, must have seemed like the end of the world. You can imagine the people – old men with turbans undone, veiled women, crying babies – tumbling out of the little bird-cage houses and down the narrow streets. Off went the minaret, as you would knock off an icicle, from the mosque on the hill. The mosque by the waterfront went down in a cloud of dust, and up from the dust, from a petrol shell, shot a geyser of fire. Stones came rumbling down from the old square tower, which had stood since the days of Bayazid; the faded grey houses squashed like eggs. It was all over in an hour – some say even twenty minutes – but that was long enough to empty Gallipoli, to kill some sixty or seventy people, and drive the rest into the caves under the cliffs by the water, or across the Marmora to Lapsaki."

Arthur Ruhl, American journalist

Western front, France, c. 1915. A crucifix behind the French front. The strategic plans of all the forces are geared towards a quick, victorious campaign. After all, every war waged in Europe after Napoleon had been over after a few months. With both generals and newspapers promising a victory before Christmas, the armies are ill-prepared for the first winter of the war.

"My dear Deern, I must tell you that I have unfortunately lost my laundry bag with all my winter clothes. Can you please send me thick socks and thick underwear? It will have to be dispatched while it isn't too cold, to make sure that the things get here during the cold weather when the post is slow. And then my dear send me cigars in little packages. The coffee cubes are very good too."

Robert Pöhland, German soldier

▶ **Russian Poland, c. 1915. Prussian artillery by the graves of fallen soldiers.** In the first month of the war Germany and France each lose 300,000 soldiers; the much smaller British professional army is almost completely wiped out. By the end of 1914, Russia and Austria have each lost a million soldiers. The figures are too terrifying to be published. Soon, it is no longer permitted to print the lists of the fallen in the newspapers.

"We joined up with three sergeants, Corporal Fourrier and a corporal to say a rosary. We said about ten, each one meant for our families. Couldn't you do the same? I feel that the rosary we say, more or less at the same time, would bring us closer together. If you like, we'll say a rosary before nine o'clock in the morning, for France, for our dead and wounded, for all those who are fighting, for all our loved ones whom we love so much and ask the Mother of God to place us under her protection. Ask Mother and Paulette to say about ten each, you say one yourself, as well as my little Madelon, who is a great girl, and I will say the other."

Alexandre Jacqueau, French soldier

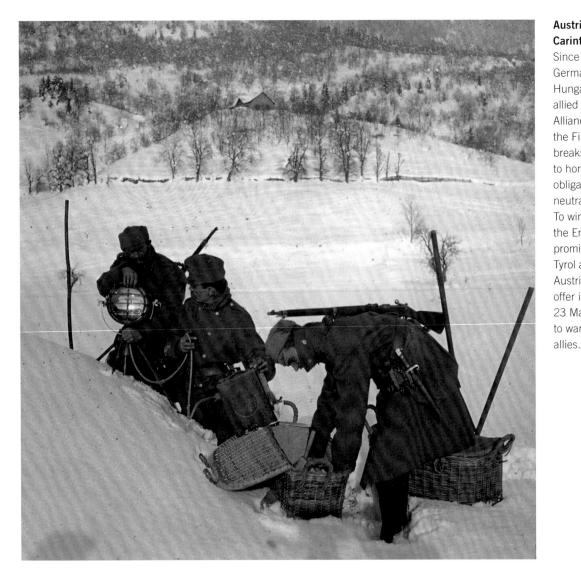

"Italy's breach of faith was received here with the same equanimity as almost everywhere in the German-speaking world. Russia's defeat must first be complete, and then it will be Italy's turn. But, even if it is defeated now, Russia will come back in fifty or a hundred years . Much later, when Germany has passed her peak, when it loses its first position in the world, only then will Russia, driven westwards by the yellow men, assume the leading role in Europe.
With cordial greetings!"

Gerrit Engelke, German soldier

Sofia, Bulgaria, 1917.
Bulgarian dignitaries
wait for Kaiser Wilhelm
II in Sofia. The example
of Bulgaria shows how
confusing allied policy
before, and during, the
First World War is. As
a Slavic country, it is
historically allied with
Russia, and thus with
the Entente. At the same
time it lays claim to
parts of Serbia, its ally
through the Entente.
The summer of 1915,
in which diplomats on
both sides are wrangling
over Bulgaria, goes
down in history as the
'Bulgarian summer'.
On 6 September 1915
Bulgaria finally makes its
decision – and invades
Serbia a month later.

"Thus ends one of the most important chapters in the history of diplomacy. The discredit for the result must be divided between Russia, but for whom Bulgaria would probably have been brought in months ago, and Serbia, whose obstinacy and cupidity have now brought her to the verge of disaster."

Herbert Asquith, British prime minister

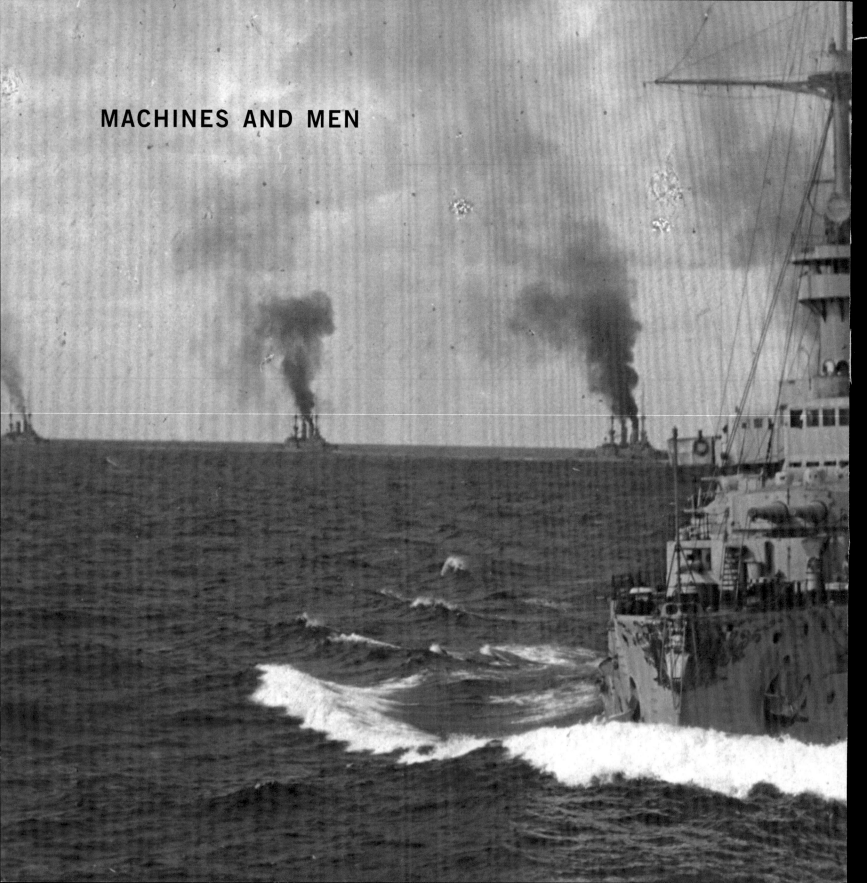

MACHINES AND MEN

"Mechanical Death went steadily on. Four Turkish batteries on the Kislar Dargh were blown up one after the other by our battleships. We watched the thick rolling smoke of the explosions, and saw bits of wheels, and the arms and legs of gunners blown up in little black fragments against that pearl-pink sunrise."

John Hargrave, British soldier in the Royal Army Medical Corps

An Austro-Hungarian dispatch cyclist. In the course of the war bicycles increasingly replace horses as means of transport.

The technical dimensions of the First World War went far beyond anything the soldiers could ever have imagined. Cartridges, grenades and gas were produced and deployed on an industrial scale, then tens of thousands of soldiers would march as though they were facing an army of knights on the other side. They were met by machine guns instead, each capable of taking on an entire regiment. In Artois, near Loos, in September 1915, more than 15,000 British infantrymen attacked while their officers shouted commands from their horses. More than half of the soldiers fell during the very first attack. When the survivors turned back at the barbed wire and fled over the field of corpses, the German soldiers felt such horror and sympathy at seeing so many dead bodies that they ceased fire.

On 24 June 1916, the British expeditionary forces on the Somme went on the offensive. For a whole week, more than 1,500 guns fire more than 1.6 million shells along a fifteen-kilometre stretch of the front, amounting to more than one hundred explosions per metre. 'The enemy was blasted by a hurricane of fire,' wrote one war reporter. The enemy was the 6th Army, consisting of predominantly Bavarian soldiers under the command of Crown Prince Rupert of Bavaria. Beneath the Germans' particularly well-fortified positions, seven underground tunnels were burrowed through the chalky soil. Twenty-four tonnes of explosive were ignited at the end of each tunnel, leaving ninety-metre wide craters in their wake. After this, it seemed impossible that there could still be human life in the enemy trenches. Twenty-one-year-old Captain Wilfred Nevill, of the Royal East Surrey Regiment, had brought four footballs back from a holiday in London, one for each of the four platoons of his company. His soldiers were to play the balls forward during the offensive, and whoever kicked them the furthest across no-man's land would get a prize: 'The Great European Cup. The Final. East Surrey vs. Bavaria. Kick off at Zero!'

A German airship division on the way to the front. Parts of their airship can be seen on the trailers.

Many of the German soldiers in the bastioned trenches were killed, but many managed to survive, albeit with their nerves completely shot, deafened by the noise and half dead from thirst. They were, however, still able to work their machine guns. When 100,000 British soldiers approached German lines, 20,000 were shot dead and 40,000 badly injured in one day. One of the first to die was Captain Wilfred Nevill. 1 July 1916 was the bloodiest day in British history, and the offensive didn't end until the final days of October. By then, 419,000 British soldiers had been killed, severely injured or captured. The French, who had attacked further south, lost almost 200,000 soldiers, the Germans 600,000. The German army also lost a further 400,000 at Verdun, where they had made the same unsuccessful attempt to break through as their opponents on the Somme. Nothing changed on the front line, at least not anything worth mentioning.

In September, the British Army employed the first armoured 'landships' on the Somme. They had been constructed despite being regarded as laughable by the officers, like 'ancient toads in the dawn of a new world era'.

British gunners taken prisoner by Austro-Hungarian troops in Montenegro. If enemy equipment is captured in such quantities, it is soon deployed against its former owners.

(*Opposite*) German soldiers extinguish a fire in Ecurey in occupied France. The German military administration assumes many duties in the occupied territories.

Winston Churchill, as First Lord of the Royal Navy, was convinced otherwise. He secretly – and illegally – financed the building of prototypes from his fleet budget. The first forty-nine vehicles were packed into crates marked with the code-name 'tank' as camouflage. This stuck, soon becoming the name for the new military equipment. Very few of them reached the third line of the German defence, but the soldiers still went into a panic as the machines rolled over the trenches. Behind the vehicles, the British infantrymen managed to advance by three kilometres. Admittedly they were forced back, but the advantages of the new equipment had been clearly proven. Commander-in-chief General Douglas Haig was so impressed that he demanded the delivery of a thousand tanks. By the time of the Allied offensive in the summer of 1918, they were technically advanced enough that the engines and gears were running reliably and the armour was able to withstand light grenade fire. For the first time, a way to advance against the machine guns had been found. On the German side, the building of tanks had been neglected, as the armament industries had been concentrating on submarines instead. By 1918, their army command was only able to employ around twenty tanks. The British built almost 1,900, and the French 4,000. In the offensives at Soissons on 18 July 1918 and at Amiens on 8 August 1918, the Germans suffered their greatest defeats since the war had broken out.

The officers of the German army had more trust in the submarine when it came to forcing Britain into submission and, ultimately, winning the war. Once the announcement was made that, from 1 February 1917, every trade ship en route to Allied docks would be sunk, they accepted that American involvement was

An Austro-Hungarian officer inspects a newly arrived troop of cyclists. At the start of the war France and Belgium are particularly reliant on specialist bicycle units.

inevitable. Many trade ships were sunk in the first few months, 458 boats in April alone. But then Britain equipped its ships with sonar devices capable of locating the submarines, and the seas began to be monitored by numerous vessels, including carriers equipped with seaplanes. The decoding of the German navy's wireless signals also helped with the discovery of submarines, and an increasing number of Allied ships and German submarines were sunk; of the 380 German submarines in operation, 187 were lost. But not a single one of the American troop carriers, which shipped two million soldiers across the Atlantic, was sunk by German submarines. The submarines had no decisive military significance; they may have obstructed Great Britain's trade links, but they didn't sever them. Given that the sinking of trade ships without warning and without the possibility of saving the seamen contravened martial law and was seen as being malicious, the instances contributed greatly to the destruction of Germany's image and confirmation of the nation's war guilt.

Planes had a far better reputation than the treacherous submarines. They did not ambush the opponent in a devious manner, and the pilots fought with equal weapons. At first, they were not used in battle, but predominantly in tactical air reconnaissance. German planes and airships, however, started dropping bombs on Paris during the Battle of the Marne of September 1914. French engineers developed planes which were equipped with machine guns, shooting down German aircraft for the first time in autumn 1914. Then the Dutch engineer Anton Fokker built a fighter plane which enabled the Germans to secure air superiority by the end of 1915. When the German attack on Verdun began in 1916, 170 planes were also employed. The Royal Air Force was founded in 1918. The following year, together with the French aircraft, it won back air superiority for the

Allies. In the 'War of the Engineers' (David Lloyd George), some of the Allied planes were already equipped with voice radio. Towards the end of the war, American planes with machine guns attacked German enemy lines, and American bombers destroyed the communication links, depots and military bases behind the front. The era of modern aerial warfare had begun.

Initially, the fighter plane still had very little to do with the anonymous mass destruction between the trenches. The names of the pilots on all sides were well known from reports of their heroic daring. Each side knew both their own aircraft, and those of their enemies. It seemed as though a piece of equipment had been found which, in place of the existing massacre, heralded the return of fairness and aristocratic spirit. The British were particularly fond of the sporting side of aerial combat, as the young

An Austro-Hungarian field kitchen division being transported to the front by railway train. Whole armies – including their supply lines – are often transported hundreds of kilometres to distant fronts.

pilot Hans Waldhausen wrote to his parents from imprisonment on 4 October 1917. He had previously shot down six planes in eight days, before being defeated by three English fighters. He survived and was taken as a prisoner of war by the British. Their officers came over to greet him with a handshake, saying: 'You're a great sportsman!'

August Fuhrmann's images of the war mainly show it as glorious and heroic, focusing on the lives of soldiers and avoiding the more harrowing aspects of the conflict; there are few photographs of battles or dead soldiers. The small size of Fuhrmann's stereoscopic cameras – compared to early film cameras – meant that it was possible to capture good photographs in the trenches themselves.

Kirchberg, Switzerland, September 1912. Even before the war – as in these manoeuvres in Switzerland in 1912 – the importance of artillery for the coming conflict is clearly apparent. The explosive power and range of modern firearms is too great for an attack on a position covered by artillery to have a good chance of success.

"Suddenly when everyone is quite naked, a light fusillade on the right of our sector.

Everyone starts running, real confusion; they ring my post and to top it all they ask me if they can speak to the artillery commander, a real theatrical scene. So I put on my cap and a pair of clogs that I had on my feet, in this garb I went to find him. It was all for the better but the sentry who was on guard had seen everything and the bad-tempered bugger exploded with laughter, and I burst out laughing as well and the commander had a good old chuckle about it too; he couldn't have done otherwise, what do you expect!"

Maurice Aupetit, French soldier

Austria, c. 1914. The Imperial German Navy is the pride of Kaiser Wilhelm II. A third of the entire German military budget is spent on the construction and maintenance of the fleet. In Britain, German rearmament is seen as a direct challenge. Though the Imperial Navy can never attain anything like the strength of the Royal Navy, German naval rearmament drives Britain to war against Germany.

"*Every year, at around the time of the first big autumn manoeuvre, fresh orders are issued to officers for the new training year beginning on 1 October. Very often for us it means bidding farewell to a beloved old weapon and moving on to a new one, or serving our supreme warlord on an unfamiliar kind of ship. It might mean moving from a liner to a torpedo boat, from the torpedo boat to a cruiser, or from a nimble cruiser to a land posting, on a revolving chair in an office, to what we call the 'paper pub'. The commander of a torpedo boat also has to be familiar with the big boys – liners and cruisers – because only someone who knows the capacity of the enemy's weapon can effectively attack their ships and finish them off.*"

German navy Lieutenant Captain Georg-Günther von Forstner, who would, during the war, become one of Germany's top submarine commanders

◄ Germany, before the war.
In 1783 the Montgolfier brothers first rise into the sky over Paris in a hot-air balloon. The storming of the heavens has begun. Hot-air balloons become airships, which enable people to travel through the air for the first time; Germany is a world leader in this new form of transport and air shows attract thousands of visitors. German airships, mainly those named after inventor Graf Zeppelin, conquer the air and shortly after the war begins, they are deployed as bombers which can strike at an enemy city silently and without warning.

"Wednesday night about eleven my husband returned to us. Well that he did, for the next morning before day had fully dawned the Zeppelins visited us! Warsaw was bombarded! Such explosions – and the return shots – people screaming – the town was alive in a moment and the exodus began. A hospital was struck and people were killed in the streets. That death dropping from the heavens – like rain on the just and the unjust – is one of the few things I could not get used to. It always left me weak and trembling and hugging my babies, hoping that if death came to us we should all go together."

Laura de Gozdawa Turczynowicz, an American woman living in Russian Poland

Amsterdam Central Station, before the war. The neutrality of the Netherlands is respected by both sides throughout the war. To stop refugees fleeing occupied Belgium to the Netherlands, German troops erect an electric fence along the border. This high-voltage obstacle kills more than two thousand people – not least because electricity is completely unknown in many villages.

"Liège, 23 June 1915.
For the making of the high voltage fence on the Belgian-Dutch border recommended by the Generalgouvernement, the following staff are required:
   a) Technical staff: dispatch of the second Landsturm Pioneer Unit: a captain, three officers, 70 NCOs and privates
   b) auxiliary staff: dispatch of armament battalion: 80 men with corresponding supervisory staff, if possible technicians as well as wood and iron workers.
   The work is predicted to take seven to eight weeks. Construction on the high voltage fence will begin on Monday the 28th of this month. Further instructions follow."

Signed, Riecke, Lieutenant Colonel

An armoured train in Galicia, 1914. Armoured trains bristling with artillery are functionally the forerunners of later tanks, though they can move only on rails.

"They yawn, and with watering eyes, in the confusion of all haste, the cries, the smoke, the roars, the lights and the flashes – far on the horizon, the terrible line of the armoured train passing."

Henri Barbusse, French author

Belgian artillery at the start of the war. The German strategy was either to march through Belgium without a fight or to conquer the little country within a few days. Instead the Belgian army keeps the German troops at bay for just over a month. King and government flee beyond the river Yser – to a little strip of Belgium that is not occupied.

"Occupied provinces are not conquered provinces. Belgium is no more a German province than Galicia is a Russian province. Nevertheless the occupied portion of our country is in a position it is compelled to endure. The greater part of our towns, having surrendered to the enemy on conditions, are bound to observe those conditions. From the outset of military operations the civil authorities of the country urged upon all private persons the necessity of abstention from hostile acts against the enemy's army. That instruction remains in force. It is our army, and our army solely, in league with the valiant troops of our Allies, that has the honour and the duty of national defence. Let us entrust the army with our final deliverance."

Désiré-Joseph, Cardinal Mercier, Archbishop of Mechelen

Dolomites, c. 1915.
Millions of soldiers suffer and die on the front, although there is no crucial victory. The true winners of the war are elsewhere; they are the owners of ammunition and arms factories. Quality standards of artillery ammunition are often very low; for example, a cargo of shells for warships, seventy per cent of which are deficient, can still be accepted. In the field, dud shells, like the one shown here, have become everyday occurrences.

"I will be spending thirteen months at the front, great sensations are blunted, great words become small, war becomes normal, service at the front a day's work, heroes become victims, volunteers chained men, life is hell, death a bagatelle, we are all cogs in a machine lurching forwards, no one knows where to, which lurches back, no one knows why, we are put at ease, honed down, dressed up, switched around, rejected – meaning has been lost, what once burned is turned to clinker, pain is leached out, the soil from which action and commitment sprouted is a barren wasteland. We throw away the pins of dud shells, out of recklessness. One of them recently went off and blew up two men, isn't everything callous?"

Ernst Toller, German writer and soldier

The German fleet in battle formation, before the war. In terms of numbers, the Royal Navy is far superior to the German Imperial Navy. For that reason the German fleet spends most of the war in the harbour. The ships do come out repeatedly, but turn around again before any clash with the superior British fleet. The navy is, however, the pride of the German Kaiser.

"Germany is a young and growing empire. It is engaged in world trade, and that trade is rapidly spreading. Germany needs a powerful fleet to protect its trade and its many interests, even on the most distant seas."

Kaiser Wilhelm II

Austrian siege artillery in Belgium, c. 1914. The Belgian army concentrates its efforts on defending the fortresses of Liège, Namur and Antwerp. Germany and its ally Austria-Hungary have to bring in heavy siege artillery to be able to conquer these fortresses.

France, winter 1915. Communication between the solders at the front and the officers in the hinterland is crucial to the success or failure of a battle. Field telephones are first used on a grand scale in the trenches of the First World War, but they are prone to failure and unreliable.

"With one or two exceptions the staff all wanted to remain in Antwerp. I myself decided to abandon the unit and stay on here as an individual or go to Ostend with the men. I think all felt as though they were running away, but it was a military order, and the Consul, the British Minister, and the King and Queen were leaving. We went to eat lunch together, and as we were doing so Mrs Stobart brought the news that the Consul had come to say that reinforcements had come up, the situation changed for the better, and for the present we might remain. We have since heard what happened. The British Minister cabled home to say that Antwerp was the key to the whole situation and must not fall, as once in here the Germans would be strongly entrenched, supplied with provisions, ammunition, and everything they want. Winston Churchill is here with Marines. They say Colonel Kitchener is at the forts."

Sarah Macnaughtan, Scottish nurse in Antwerp

"We made our way back slowly, and eventually caught the gleam of steel helmets. They were British. We had stumbled upon our left sector. We found out then that the line curved and that instead of the left sector being directly to the left of ours – the centre – it was to the left and to the rear. Also, there was a telephone wire running from one to the other. We reported and made our way back to the centre in about five minutes by feeling along the wire. That was our method afterwards, and the patrol was cushy for us."

R. Derby Holmes, American volunteer in the British Army

◄ **German warship, before the war.**
With the arms race between the British and German fleets, as well as the armament of the Austrian Navy, it appeared at the start of the war that the high seas were to be a crucial theatre of war. But as the German fleet stayed in harbour in the face of superior British power, the Royal Navy's warships are soon found a new task. As marine artillery they are to destroy the strong Turkish lines of defence on the Gallipoli Peninsula – and cover the landing of their own troops.

"*Mechanical Death went steadily on. Four Turkish batteries on the Kislar Dargh were blown up one after the other by our battleships. We watched the thick rolling smoke of the explosions, and saw bits of wheels, and the arms and legs of gunners blown up in little black fragments against that pearl-pink sunrise. The noise of Mechanical Battle went surging from one side of the bay to the other – it swept round suddenly with an angry rattle of Maxims and the hard echoing crackle of rifle-fire. Now and then our battleships crashed forth, and their shells went hurtling and screaming over the mountains to burst with a muffled roar somewhere out of sight.*"

John Hargrave, British soldier in the Royal Army Medical Corps

Russia, during the war. Artillery soldiers with their weapons on the way to the front. The First World War has etched itself into our collective memory as a battle between soldiers in the trenches. But by far the most devastating weapon in this war is artillery. This is particularly true of the many siege battles during the war.

"*The siege, so far as we were concerned, now entered on a second stage. The exhilaration bred of the novelty of being invested had by now worn off, and was succeeded for a time by the dull ache of disappointment at the failure of our people to relieve us after six weeks, and by a period of enhanced discomfort. Our unbounded faith in their capacity to help us was somewhat shaken, and although we felt quite certain of relief in the near future, yet the knowledge that it was possible for a British Relieving Force to do less than the anxiety of a besieged one had marked out for it to do, served to render our enforced confinement more irritating.*"

Charles Harrison Barber, British soldier under siege in Kut Al Amara

Eastern front, Germany, c. 1916. The longer and more hopeless the battle in the trenches becomes, the crazier were the plans for breaking the stalemate. More guns, heavier artillery – such as these mine launchers – poison gas, massed infantry – the diabolical concept of materiel warfare, focusing on massive amounts of both machinery and men, is born in the summer of 1916 in the battles of Verdun and the Somme.

"Now the ceremony was ended, and once again we set out for the front. It was to an artillery observation post that we were bound. In front of us lay a vast plain, scarred and slashed, with bare places at intervals, such as you see where gravel pits break a green common. Not a sign of life or movement, save some wheeling crows. And yet down there, within a mile or so, is the population of a city. Away to the right is a small red house, dim to the eye but clear in the glasses, which is suspected as a German post. It is to go up this afternoon. '"Mother" will soon do her in,' remarks the gunner boy cheerfully. 'Mother' is the name of the gun. 'Give her five six three four,' he cries through the 'phone. 'Mother' utters a horrible bellow from somewhere on our right. An enormous spout of smoke rises ten seconds later from near the house. 'A little short,' says our gunner. 'Two and a half minutes left. Raise her seven five,' says our boy. 'Mother' roars more angrily than ever. A flash of fire on the house, a huge pillar of dust and smoke. The German post has gone up."

Arthur Conan Doyle, British author

An excerpt from the *London Illustrated News,* **3 May 1913.** The world's first illustrated weekly news magazine. There were entire series like this, detailing how a possible war with Germany might be fought. What makes these so interesting is the fact that they were published at a time when at least the German government considered the United Kingdom a possible ally, or, at the very least, neutral, should war break out in mainland Europe.

▶ **An air show in Germany, before the war.** An arms race starts between the Entente and the Central Powers over the continuing existence of aerial reconnaissance. Each army needs to defend its own observation balloons – anti-aircraft guns and fighter pilots are used to intercept enemy planes.

"I wasn't even prepared to zoom off, when the pilot fired the engine and the plane started moving. Faster and faster, faster and faster. I clung on for dear life. All of a sudden the shaking stopped and the plane was in the air. The ground sped away from under me."

Manfred von Richthofen,
German pilot

An air show in Germany, before the war. Observation balloons are used from the start of the trench warfare. 'Reconnaissance by aircraft' is still difficult, since aeroplanes are not yet powerful or, more importantly, stable enough to serve as reliable viewing platforms. The balloons rise above their own lines, thus being protected against attack, and offer an ideal platform from which to spy on enemy positions. In order to combat observation balloons, both the Entente and the Central Powers send their best fighter planes over enemy territory.

"We decided to drop a bomb on an observation balloon, 'the' observation balloon of the Russians. We were able to go down comfortably to a few hundred metres and bomb the observation balloon. At first it was hastily pulled in, but once the bomb had fallen the pulling stopped. My explanation was not that I might have scored a hit, but that the Russians had abandoned their hetman up there in the basket and run away."

Manfred von Richthofen, German pilot

On the Western Dvina, Russian Poland, c. 1916. Air altitude above the battlefields of the First World War changes again and again in the course of the war. It isn't only a battle between pilots, but also a battle between engineers. The Dutch aeroplane manufacturer Fokker, making planes for Germany, invents the interrupter gear, which enables the pilot to fire at the enemy through his own propeller, and for months gives Germany command in the air on the western front.

"I got up at 4 am and went to the aerodrome. I set out to patrol the lines from Souchez to Arras to Sommecourt. It was a bit cloudy and on our first trip down from Souchez we had just passed Arras and crossed the lines before we knew it. As a gentle reminder that there was a war on, I heard a series of whizzes, followed by a series of bangs. I looked around to see who was doing the celebrating, and saw about a dozen shells burst about twenty yards above me. Just before eight o'clock, when I was to leave, my engine stopped, and I turned in towards our side. I looked behind and saw the archies [anti-aircraft guns] come up and blow off just behind me. I laughed at them, as they were the last efforts before I got out of reach. I left Arras at eight, and came home."

John Bernhard Prophy, Canadian pilot in France

France, 1918. From the very start, the war in the air is dominated by the flying aces on both sides. A flying ace is someone who has shot down at least five enemy planes or balloons. Pilots like the 'Red Baron', Manfred von Richthofen, Hermann Göring, the British airman Albert Ball, Frenchman Adolphe Pégoud and American Eddie Rickenbacker become celebrated stars of propaganda in their homelands.

"'He must go down, come what may!' There, a favourable moment at last. The enemy has apparently lost me and is flying straight ahead. In the fragment of a second I'm right behind him in my trusty plane. A brief burst from my machine gun. I was so close that I was afraid I would ram him. Then suddenly, I nearly whooped with joy, because the enemy's propeller had stopped turning. Hurrah! A hit!"

Manfred von Richthofen, German pilot

France, c. 1917. The expansion of the war into the air – and the subsequent ability of the enemy to pinpoint positions for artillery attack – leads to the construction of decoy gun emplacements by all the armies. These are supposed to provoke the enemy to attack, thus giving away their artillery position, which can then be destroyed. In the Austrian army such 'dummy positions' are even manned like normal artillery. For the soldiers involved this can amount to a suicide mission.

"Dummy positions are either used in fours as 'dummy gun batteries' or in twos as 'dummy gun trains' or singly. Their use is supposed to distract the attention and fire of the enemy artillery from one's own real batteries, and towards the dummy positions. In this way they are supposed to deceive and mislead the enemy commanders and their reconnaissance men (including pilots) into seeing the dummy positions as real gun emplacements. To achieve this as definitely and completely as possible, and in the long term, it usually isn't enough just to set the dummy positions up; they must be able to simulate the firing of real artillery by shooting ammunition; the firing position of the dummy emplacement must also be chosen appropriately."

The Austrian Army's 'Instructions for the installation and use of firing dummy emplacements'

Germany, before the war. In January 1915 the first German airships appear over Great Britain. The term 'Zeppelin' refers only to one manufacturer of airships; there were, in fact, several. The big advantage of airships is that at the start of the war they fly so high that enemy planes can't reach them. Their crucial disadvantage is they can only carry small payloads, so their effect on the course of the war is largely psychological.

"Eleven o'clock, a warm, moonlit night, we ascend in Cologne and follow the railway line to Aachen. We have 900 kilos of bombs, a heavy load for the ship. We left the machine guns at home, but the crew are armed with automatic rifles and pistols. Before Antwerp the clouds grow thinner and finally disappear completely. Lest we be too easy a target for the artillery of the fortress, we have to wait until the moon has gone down."

Ernst A. Lehmann, captain of a German Zeppelin

Germany, before the war.
Airships are used by both the German army and navy. In total, over 51 missions are flown, with 557 people being killed in attacks by German airships. The true effect of the deployment is that Britain has to invest a great deal of money in anti-aircraft systems – money that is not available for equipping soldiers at the front.

"On 17 March 1915 the weather improved, the radio announcement repeats: 'Attack on London.' In the faint glow through the chink I see the bombs hanging like rows of pears from the release mechanism; aside from explosive bombs of between 58 and 300 kilograms in weight, there are also phosphorus bombs, which are supposed to start fires where they land. Those malicious projectiles have not yet been activated, but still my bomb officer lies on his belly and peers impatiently through the open flap. He is a genial chap, and in peacetime he couldn't hurt a fly, but now he is itching to drop his murderous load. We are in battle, and battle knows only harshness against the enemy, who pays us back in the same coin."

Ernst A. Lehmann, captain of a German Zeppelin

Modern air-to-air encounters are not unlike medieval jousting; here man fights against man. There is an unwritten code of honour among fighter pilots who fight their battles before the eyes of countless spectators in the trenches. In the course of the war they are also deployed as reconnaissance men and equipped with cameras for the purpose.

"Only a very, very practised eye can observe anything in particular from such an altitude. I have good eyes, but it seems dubious to me whether there is anyone at all who can recognize anything precise from an altitude of five thousand metres. So one must depend on something else which replaces the eye, and that is the photographic camera. So one photographs everything which one considers important, and which one is supposed to photograph."

Manfred von Richthofen, German pilot

A destroyed bridge across the Isonzo river, Austrian-Italian front, 1917. In the valley of the Isonzo river, Italy and Austria-Hungary fight a total of twelve fierce battles in the course of the First World War. Despite horrendous losses, the first eleven battles do not bring either side any major territorial gains. The Allied plan is to keep German and Austrian armies tied up in these battles and away from the fronts in France and Russia.

"While the Italians had, with laudable courage in the course of ten Isonzo battles, previously kept encroaching bravely into Austrian positions, the picture suddenly changed when seven divisions from Upper Silesia, Brandenburg, Württemberg and Bavaria appeared among the Austrian ranks at Tolmein. It was as it had been in Bukovina, when the pointed helmets of a Prussian cavalry division appeared in front of the victorious Russians, and the horrified cry of 'Germanski' made the rounds. The Habsburg sloppiness was swept away by German confidence, one karst mountain after another bore the German flag on its summit, 5 Italian Army completely destroyed (700 guns., 80,000 casualties), 2 A. rolled up, from 22 Oct until 1 Dec. Italy's defeat was sealed, it could have been greater if the Austrians had done more. To keep Italy in the alliance, an English auxiliary corps under Plumer was sent, France even wanted to send 15 divisions. As a result some of the west's supremacy, which had previously been rising, was lost because considerable German forces were diverted to the Isonzo."

Karl August Bleibtreu, German author

"Next night we were billeted at Barlin – don't get that mixed up with Berlin, it's not the same – in an abandoned convent within range of the German guns. The roar of artillery was continuous and sounded pretty close. Now and again a shell would burst nearby with a kind of hollow 'spung', but for some reason we didn't seem to mind. I had expected to get the shivers at the first sound of the guns and was surprised when I woke up in the morning after a solid night's sleep."

R. Derby Holmes, American volunteer in the British Army

Dolomites, c. 1916. Alongside the different kinds of shells, there are also the different calibres of heavy, medium and light artillery. This mortar is being mounted on the Dolomite front. The soldiers soon learn to recognize calibres and types of shell from the noise they make.

Russian Poland, c. 1916. Captured Russian guns on display. The longer the war lasts, the longer there are no clear victors, the more important smaller successes become. The seizure of enemy material provides fodder for propaganda, as well as a source of great pride for the soldiers who acquired the 'booty'.

"The eight-inchers struck ear more than the fifteen-inchers. The discharge of the fifteen-inch exactly like my bombing explosion – the splash of flame occupying your whole sight, the push of a hot wind, and the world-filling sound and vibration of everything. Showers of bits of cardboard fly back after the discharge. Eat our sandwiches in car and then go on."

C.E. Montague, British war correspondent

"Not many dead on the battlefield of yesterday; only single bodies; no groups. I only see one dead British soldier. Several batteries of enemy field-guns standing where they were captured, with the name of the capturing infantry brigade carefully chalked on them. Ground and road little shell-marked, nothing like Somme in 1916."

C.E. Montague, British war correspondent

France, c. 1916. Enemy armies depend on weapons that are usually very different in detail. One reason for this is so that captured material – like these rubber wheels – cannot easily be put to use by the enemy against one's own troops. But if soldiers capture enemy firearms and grenades, of course they use these.

"*Near Authuille I hand over my seven prisoners to the officer in charge of a collecting-place. We find the enemy trenches on the Thiepval ridge to have been left suddenly. Everything left as it was – rifles, equipment, a prayer-book, many letters, revolvers, a Very light (which I lost), etc.*"

C.E. Montague, British war correspondent

Outside Warsaw, Polish Russia, 1915. The machine gun – here a German model in an emplacement – is the primary defensive weapon of trench warfare. The machine guns used in the First World War, built into fixed positions, make it impossible for the enemy to cross no-man's-land.

"For France! Forward! I saw no one hesitating to charge – over the top they went, bayonets at the ready. I see them running towards a terrifying blaze, they were still flying, lost in the hurricane, mown down by cannon or machine gun, their deaths are glorious. They have spilled their blood for our freedom. Fallen in the field of honour, they have made their choice. Those accursed murderers, that imperial guard with only brute force at its disposal. I salute you! You who fell, rifle in hand, your example yesterday will serve its purpose tomorrow."

Maurice Aupetit, French soldier

Western front, France, winter 1915. Like artillery, machine guns fire huge quantities of ammunition. Maintaining supply lines is even more important for machine-gun positions, because they are in the front line. If a gun runs out of ammunition, the enemy can advance unhindered.

Dardanelles, Turkey, 18 March 1915. To end the war against the Ottoman Empire quickly, Great Britain sends a fleet of battleships which are to pass through the Dardanelles and attack Constantinople. But the fleet comes under fire from heavy land artillery and is beaten back.

"At one point in the action, we witnessed the assault by two 75 mm guns, by a German infantry company. Those two guns were defended by about twenty artillerymen. The German unit attacked in serried ranks, four abreast and to the sound of fifes. Our enemies only know how to fight in serried ranks, which explains the considerable number of their losses. It's the opposite of the French soldier, who fights much better in a scattered organization because he needs all his initiative. From a distance of 200 metres, our soldiers received them with dense, repeated fire, then at 100 metres, since our artillerymen had run out of grapeshot, fired millinite bullets at the crowd. It was terrifying. Our boches leapt seven or eight metres in the air and were all blown to pieces. There were hardly any members of the unit left, I assure you, and they didn't put up much resistance."

Alexandre Jacqueau, French soldier

"When the ships pushed on up the strait toward Kilid Bahr and Chanak Kale – somewhat like trying to run the Narrows at New York – there was a different story. They were now within range of shore batteries and there were anchored mines and mines sent down on the tide. On March 18 the Irresistible, Ocean, and Bouvet were sunk, and it began to be apparent that the Dardanelles could not be forced without the help of a powerful land force. So in April landing parties were sent ashore."

Arthur Ruhl, American journalist

Outside Warsaw, Polish Russia, 1915. To break the stalemate in the trenches, the armies of both the Entente and the Central Powers often dig tunnels far under enemy lines. The finished tunnels are filled with explosives and then blown up, along with the enemy trench crew above them. The explosion is followed by a major attack which seeks to break through the resulting hole in enemy lines.

"Arriving at Cassel at eleven last night, I leave at midnight with P. Phillips, Gibbs, Sims, and Small to see the Messines Ridge battle from the Scherpenberg. Reach it about one. Watch the lazy lights and sullen sounds of the front for half an hour and then go to sleep under a hedge. Next thing I am aware of, through a film of sleep, is a light whimper of shrapnel bursting somewhere near. Just after, I am fully awaked by the rocking of the hill under me. I jump up, sagely thinking it must be an earthquake, and then see seven huge mines still exploding – geysers of flame with black objects in it, leaving huge palm-trees of smoke drifting away in file."

C.E. Montague, British war correspondent

Italian Alps, c. 1916. An Austrian artillery emplacement in the mountains. Whether in the battlefields of Belgium or France or, as here, in the Alps, the destruction wrought by war is so complete that nothing remains of the previous landscape. In the war between Italy and Austria-Hungary, a whole mountain peak is blown up at Col di Lana, for example, while artillery in France and Belgium repeatedly level entire ridges.

"I have the busiest, oddest time. In the afternoon I may be on a recent battlefield, with the flies still completing the work of clearing away the remnants, and the same evening at a French country house of the late sixteenth century in an idyllic pastoral place, with not a sound at night. You can't conceive the completeness of the destruction made by our latest artillery arrangements and I never heard in the trenches anything like the cannonading that goes on now even on a relatively quiet day. All the better – it is the only way to the end."

C.E. Montague, British war correspondent, in a letter to his wife

A German gun in Malancourt, France, c. 1915. No soldier can endure the war at the front for long. Precise timetables vary, but soldiers often spend a day at the front, then a day in the hinterland. On the other hand, for the first years of the war in France, there is no real home leave at all.

"My dear Jakob,
Now that we have finally put the Somme behind us, I can write again. On 21 October (my birthday) we had to survive our fiercest day of artillery fire and hold off an English attack. My inner certainty was not deceptive – I came out of it safe and sound. Many did not.
It can't be long now until leave! You have no idea how much I'm looking forward to it!
Goodbye!"

Gerrit Engelke, German worker poet and soldier

Carinthia, Austria, 1915. An Austrian sentry in the mountains looks down on enemy positions. The power of the artillery on both sides in the First World War makes one thing clear above all: survival depends entirely on chance. Neither courage nor bravery nor caution count for anything. A shell can hit anyone – at any time.

"Then the order came in to storm the mountain opposite. As we advanced and the enemy noticed that we wanted to launch an attack, they set fire to the houses so that they could see what we were trying to do. We couldn't attack, so the order came to 'halt', or the whole regiment would be killed. Everyone was to dig in where he stood and await further instructions. At midnight everyone dug as best they could to protect themselves. At dawn the Russians realized that something must have gone wrong for us, and had their artillery shoot at our slope. We crept into our holes as best we could. The firing intensified all the more. The shots fell about twenty paces behind us. All we could do was huddle up as best we could. Our artillery started firing. Then a barrage began. Soil flew into the trenches as if someone was shovelling it in. We were almost deafened by the fire, and thought our last hour had come. Everything was completely dark in front of our eyes for all the smoke. And we couldn't do anything, we could only watch."

Karl Kasser, Austrian soldier

Vingré, France, c. 1916. Since the first German attack with chlorine gas on 22 April 1914, poison gas has been one of the most feared weapons of war. The French had used tear gas in August 1914, but chlorine, often fatal, escalates gas warfare – and lays the foundation for the use of still more gases on both sides. To make contaminated positions inhabitable again after a gas attack, the French army uses Vermorel canisters. These release a neutralizing mixture of chemicals that are supposed to remove the poison gas.

"One thing that was done after the August attack was definitely and finally to withdraw the Vermorel sprayers for use for clearing the gas out of the trenches and dugouts. These instruments, brought up for the work of spraying fruit trees and vineyards, had done some first-class fighting of the German gas, right in the front line, as long as the gas was chlorine. But with the introduction of large quantities of phosgene the work of the sprayers was gone. They could not touch the phosgene, and consequently Tommy's dependence on them was a snare and made things more dangerous for him than if they had not been used at all. For a dugout might be sprayed and thought, therefore, to be quite healthy to sleep in and yet contain as much phosgene as would at any rate cause minor and delayed effects."

Major Samuel Johnson Mason Auld, Royal Berkshire Regiment

France, 1917. A new Schneider CA1 tank at the front. The first tanks were developed in Britain during the First World War. To keep the invention secret, they were originally called 'land-ships', but were then renamed 'water-carriers', or tanks for short. The first tanks had no cannon, but were primarily a way of crossing no-man's-land while being protected against machine guns and barbed wire entanglements.

"We came to an expanse where many monsters were clumsily cavorting like dinosaurs in primeval slime. These were the far-famed tanks. Their commander, or chief mahout – as I was inclined to call him – was a cheerful young giant of colonial origin. He had been expecting us, and led me to where one of these leviathans was awaiting us. You crawl through a greasy hole in the bottom, and the inside is as full of machinery as the turret of the Pennsylvania, *and you grope your way to the seat in front beside that of the captain and conductor, looking out through a slot in the armour over a waste of water and mud. From here you are supposed to operate a machine gun. Behind you two mechanics have started the engines with a deafening roar, above which are heard the hoarse commands of the captain as he grinds in his gears."*

Winston Churchill, American journalist

France, 1917. In their first battles – as in the baptism of fire of the French Schneider CA tank at Berry-au-Bac on 16 April 1917 – the early tanks are hopelessly overtaxed. They are poorly conceived, their crews inexperienced. Breakdowns and accidents ensure that only very few tanks make it to the front. But as the tanks become more efficient, the more the previously unprotected infantrymen value the cover the tanks provide.

"There was a tank just ahead of me. I got behind it. And marched there. Slow! God, how slow! Anyhow, it kept off the machine-gun bullets, but not the shrapnel. It was breaking over us in clouds. I felt the stunning patter of the fragments on my tin hat, cringed under it, and wondered vaguely why it didn't do me in. I thought we must be nearly there and sneaked a look around the edge of the tank. A traversing machine gun raked the mud, throwing up handfuls, and I heard the gruff 'row, row' of flattened bullets as they ricocheted off the steel armour. I ducked back, and on we went. I don't suppose that trip across no-man's-land behind the tanks took over five minutes, but it seemed like an hour."

R. Derby Holmes, American volunteer in the British Army

France, during the war. Officers view new armoured cars and mobile artillery. Armoured cars are considerably more widespread in the First World War than 'real' tanks. They are not suitable for use in muddy no-man's-land, because of their wheels, designed for road use.

"Reisiger and Schmidt's anti-tank guns were close to Blerancourt. Apart from the two officers, the unit consisted of: junior field doctor Winkel, two NCOs, ten gunners and three telephone operators. The two guns had been put into position on a quiet night, with no losses. They were positioned in the open field. A roof of wire mesh heaped with leaves protected it against being seen from the air. Firing the guns was expressly forbidden. They were only to be fired directly at armoured cars as a shock tactic."

Edlef Köppen, German soldier

▶ **North Sea, Germany, before the war.** The mighty war fleets of Britain and Germany spend most of the war in their harbours – the German fleet seen here and in the following pages during a fleet review that took place before the war, complete with simulated combat. Most fighting on the sea is done with smaller ships. The Germans rely above all on their new weapon, the submarine.

"'Torpedo at the ready!' With a firm hand the gunner stands by the trigger of the torpedo tube. A single brief order from the mouth of his commander will free him from his tension. Just one brief word and his grip on the trigger will free the torpedo from the tube and send it on its way to the hated, still unsuspecting enemy, before drilling itself deep into its steel body with a violent explosion."

Georg-Günther von Forstner, German submarine commander

The Baltic Sea off Kiel, Germany, before the war. The fleets of Germany and Britain clash only once, on 31 May 1916 – in the Battle of Jutland. The sailors on both sides, who have until that point spent most of the war in the harbour or on patrol, suddenly find themselves in the middle of a battle for life or death.

"*I must say it's very different from what I expected. I expected to be excited but was not a bit; it's hard to express what we did feel like, but you know the sort of feeling one has when one goes in to bat at cricket and rather a lot depends upon you doing well and you're waiting for the first ball; well, it's very much the same as that – do you know what I mean? To start with, it was all at such long range that the destroyers were rather out of it, except there were plenty of fifteen-inch falling round us, and we just watched. It really seemed rather like a battle practice on a large scale, and we could see the flashes of the German guns on the horizon.*"

Anonymous British officer aboard a destroyer in the Battle of Jutland

The Baltic Sea off Kiel, Germany, before the war. Most of the German fleet has enticed part of the British fleet into a trap. A big German victory seems certain – when suddenly the main body of the Royal Navy arrives. The German fleet is greatly outnumbered – and has to flee.

"*Our first news that there had been a battle was the German Wireless message that announced to the world that 'a portion' of their High Sea Fleet had met our Grand Fleet in full force and had defeated it. Presently we got various single 'intercepts' between Sir David Beatty and the Commander-in-Chief of the Grand Fleet referring to losses of various ships. The damaged ships began to come into East Coast ports with many hospital cases on board. Of course, wild rumours were flying about all over the country, since officers and men were wiring to their friends saying that they were all right. There was normally no censorship of inland messages, but on this occasion messages of the nature indicated were held up for inquiry before being sent on.*"

Sir Douglas Brownrigg, British naval censor

The Baltic Sea off Kiel, Germany, before the war. In the confusion of the night, the German fleet is able to escape, even sinking several British ships. By the end, the German navy has sunk fourteen vessels, losing eleven of its own. A tactical victory – yet the German fleet returns to harbour, which it won't leave until the end of the war.

"*Utterly mistaking the situation, a large enemy cruiser with four funnels came up at 2 am (apparently one of the Cressy class), and was soon within 1,500 metres of Squadron I's battleships, the* Thuringen *and* Ostfriesland. *In a few seconds she was on fire, and sank with a terrible explosion four minutes after opening fire. The destruction of this vessel, which was so near that the crew could be seen rushing backwards and forwards on the burning deck while the searchlights disclosed the flight of the heavy projectiles till they fell and exploded, was a grand but terrible sight.*"

Reinhard Scheer, German vice-admiral

The Baltic Sea off Kiel, Germany, before the war. After the Battle of Jutland, the giant German and British fleets spend most of the war in their harbours. To protect them there, both sides lay big barriers in the form of minefields. As a result, only the navies that had laid the mines knew where they were, and were consequently able to put into harbour.

"The fleet was still outside. At about three o'clock we heard vigorous gunfire, but it could just have been manoeuvres. Then a torpedo boat was said to have run into our mines near Schillig, where Gluckauf lay at anchor. We received an order to escort a medical ship through the lines, but then in the thick fog we couldn't find the ship. The task was a serious one, we were so agitated that there was chaos. Then the order came to steam slowly for Schillig and look for drifting mines, and perhaps to shoot them with our cannon."

Joachim Ringelnatz, German sailor and author

Trench near Hollebeke, Belgium, c. 1916. German soldiers examine the state of the ammunition in their trench. For the soldiers, battles are often only brief intermezzos between endless pauses in which they and their enemies lie opposite one another in their respective trenches.

"Dear Désirée,
We are in the front-line trenches, one man was killed last night by a rifle cartridge and two were wounded.
I received your parcel, it arrived at just the right time because we had nothing left to eat that day.
I went up on to the plain twice yesterday to put up some wire, but lots of rifle cartridges came down and we had to go back into our shelters.
By day, those sales boches don't say anything, but they don't stop firing shells and shell-torpedoes.
Your friend for ever."

Auguste 'Maurice' Lecourt, French soldier

Germany, 1914. At the beginning of the First World War, Germany relies more than any other belligerent nation on submarines. It becomes apparent just how unprepared the other countries are for German submarine attacks on 22 September, when the U9 sinks the British armoured cruisers HMS *Hogue,* HMS *Aboukir* and HMS *Cressy.* In the course of the war commercial vessels bound for Great Britain increasingly find themselves in the sights of the submarines.

Western front, c. 1917. Massive artillery placements like these testify to the vast costs that the endless war involves. Throughout the war the Entente spends on average around 36,000 dollars to kill an enemy soldier. Germany is more effective; the cost here is only about 11,000 dollars.

"So we lay in wait in the English Channel. At last a big steamer appeared behind us. We had an Englishman in front of us! Even after we fired our warning shots he didn't stop his ship, but fired off flares that were supposed to summon English patrol vessels. We had no choice but to bring his ship to a standstill. His only answer was to raise the red British ensign, in a sign that he wanted to fight. Fine! Constantly turning in a circle, the Englishman tried to ram us. Each time, a loud explosion told him how trigger-happy our gunners can be. A well-aimed shot struck the Englishman's flagpole, so that the flag came down, but a short time afterwards it was hoisted again on ship's foremast. The very next hit brought it down again. It rose a third time on a remaining halyard. But in the confusion it was flown upside down, with the union jack at the bottom, and flying like that it accompanied the brave ship into the depths."

Lieutenant Captain Georg-Günther von Forstner, commander of German submarine U14

"As long as Johnny Frenchman and John Bull have money, the Americans will be happy to send them powder and lead and mines, until the war ends, promptly, and the neutral ones are the only sensible people in the world. Everything's already forgotten here. There was no point in so many people having to die. We are still in the same spot as before. Four to five hundred thousand marks is not a small amount, just for ammunition that we fire off in three hours."

Carl Schmidt, German soldier, about an artillery attack

Menen, Belgium, c. 1915. The whole economy is put at the service of the war not just here, in conquered Belgium, but everywhere in the belligerent countries. For all the hundreds of thousands of dead at the front, there are war profiteers at home, enriched by every shell fired.

"A stench of blood surrounds these supposedly respectable businessmen. Whether they came from the land of unlimited possibilities or from the empire of peach-blossom – none of them had ever heard the swallow-twitter of a bullet, or seen the solemnly frozen, pale yellow face and fists crossed over the chest of a fallen man. They knew nothing of bloody straw and screams and the flickering glow of a night-time bandaging station in a shattered church, but only the dry jokes of congenial visitors to the stock market. Their Gardens of Eden blossomed out of poison gas and infernal machines. From the tears of widows and orphans they created the pearls for their wives and daughters. The high-altitude euphoria of the immeasurable exploitation of the giant Russian empire fevered in the cold eyes of England and her vassals."

Rudolph Heinrich Stratz, German writer

SUFFERING

> "At the start of the campaign, only a very few went to mass, many behaved in an uncouth manner, relieving themselves in the cemeteries adjacent to the churches and several times in the churches themselves. Today, the churches are too small to contain all the people who want to go to service."

Alexandre Jacqueau, French soldier

In the summer and autumn of 1916, the Battle of the Somme killed or badly injured 1.2 million combatants. And it was all for nothing: by the end of the year there was still no victory, still no ray of hope. Even to this day, the battle is regarded as the greatest military tragedy in British history. Cemeteries now mark the front line of 1916, and wreaths and flowers are still laid down by family members.

In Germany, it was abundantly clear that only a swift victory on the western front and then in the east could end the war. When the capture of Paris failed and the German troops were stopped at the Marne, they initially retreated to the trenches. They occupied strategically placed mountain slopes and set up heavy machine guns that they soon cemented to the floor. The situation didn't change much from then until 1918, apart from the fact that millions died in mostly failed attacks on the enemy's barbed wire and trenches.

German soldiers receive their food rations in a camp in the forest on the eastern front. Through lack of hygiene – particularly in the preparation of food – illnesses can spread like wildfire among the troops.

The retreat of the Germans from the Marne led to growing euphoria amongst the British and French officers in 1914. The British General Henry Wilson estimated that the German border would be breached in four weeks' time, which meant victory by Christmas. But by December, it was realized that there was no end in sight. The horrific extent of this European slaughter was becoming clear. In the first five months, almost a million French soldiers had been killed or so badly injured that they had to be withdrawn from the battlefield. On the German side, the losses amounted to around 750,000. The numbers in Austria-Hungary were around the same. The British forces had lost 300,000 soldiers in just three months, amounting to two-thirds of their number.

Tributes were paid to victims of the Great War in all countries. They were – and continue to be – seen as heroes, and memorials and days of remembrance were established. The severely injured survivors remained constantly visible, however, carrying a less heroic image of the war home with them. With their maimed faces and limbs, they shocked those on the home front so much that, in Hamburg for example, they were banned from entering the Jungfernstieg railway station.

Wounded Austro-Hungarian troops at a school converted into a field hospital. If a village or a town is taken, buildings must quickly be found to treat the wounded. These are generally churches and schools.

And yet there had been so much optimism at the start of the war that the 'triumph of the machine' in modern warfare would protect the individual. The chances of coming home uninjured were supposed to have been greater than ever before, as the *Breisgauer Zeitung* claimed on 1 August. High-speed shots would be fired into the body without causing any great damage, the newspaper had said; the wound could then, allegedly, be easily treated and healed. But in the trenches it was, mostly, the hailstorm of shrapnel that tore the soldiers' bodies to shreds. And the surgeons were unable to give any more than the most basic of treatment, for they had hundreds of thousands of patients to tend to.

Fuhrmann describes this picture from the village of Strzałkowo, in the German-occupied part of Poland, as 'a gallery of beautiful Polish girls' – although they are standing behind a barrier of bars and barbed wire.

After Russian troops conquered the city of Gródek in Galicia in September 1914, medical assistant Georg Trakl tried in vain to prevent many maimed soldiers from dying. He was moved to write *Grodek*, his last poem ever before he himself died:

> *Yet a red cloud silently gathers over the pastures,*
> *An angry God, spilled blood itself*
> *Dwelling within, a moonlike coolness;*
> *All roads seep into black decay*

In Germany, there were 2.7 million 'war cripples' walking the streets. People were also horrified by the 200,000 'war neurotics', particularly the 'shakers' or 'tremblers' who had survived shelling and detonations in the trenches and who were constantly grimacing, twitching and flailing their arms about. They were treated with electric shocks in the clinics, which only made them worse. According to a government medical report, in Germany there were more than 600,000 soldiers who had been diagnosed as psychologically ill. But given that they were regarded as being curable, they had no claim to an injured person's pension. The British authorities, on the other hand, recognized the effects of shell shock and provided around 50,000 veterans with a state pension.

The psychologically ill in Germany strayed into a difficult trap when, in 1934, they put their trust in the promises of the 'Act regarding Procedures in Insurance Matters' and applied for pensions. The applications were denied, but collected in the records of 'hereditary defectives'. During 'Action T4' in 1940 and 1941, when psychologically and physically ill victims were murdered, even the war disabled ended up on the 'euthanasia' lists. By the time the protests of Catholic priests and some nurses forced the abandonment of the murders, 250 of them had already been killed. The Bishop of Münster, Clemens August von Galen, cleverly drew attention to the murder of war veterans in his sermons.

Joseph Goebbels was enraged by this, cursing over the 'dagger in the back of the fighting front'.

The offensives of the First World War resulted in prisoners of war whose numbers reached into the hundreds of thousands. According to the rules of war, they had to be adequately nourished and could not be employed for military purposes. Despite this, they suffered from a lack of food and clothing, and were used for heavy labour everywhere. Thousands of British detainees worked alongside Russian prisoners of war in the Baltic forests, where millions of cubic metres of wood were felled for the fortification of the trenches on the western front.

The media in all the countries involved began to report on the bad treatment of their own prisoners of war in other countries. The Bavarian Higher Regional Court Judge Müller-Meiningen stated in the heading of a pamphlet that: 'Treatment of German prisoners

A group of prisoners of war. Fuhrmann identifies some of the wounded Russian soldiers as Circassians. Whether they ever saw their home again is unknown.

abroad contravenes international law. Exemplary treatment of prisoners in Germany'. The result was that, by pointing to the enemy's abuses of prisoners, the treatment of one's own prisoners of war became increasingly violent. To start with, prisoners of war were brought back behind the fronts; then the Germans began to deploy prisoners on the front in fortification missions. French and British prisoners were employed on the eastern front, Russian soldiers on the western front. French army units took Germans to Africa with them, while British units employed Germans on the front in France. Everywhere, prisoners were made to dig trenches in the midst of grenade fire. H. J. Clarke, a British prisoner of war in the Giessen camp, noted the following in his journal: 'On 14 January 1917, 580 men left Giessen to work behind the German lines, and 260 returned.' A French prisoner of war wrote to his wife that they were treated 'not like soldiers, but slaves'.

Captured officers, however, were treated well everywhere. Only for them were the old virtues of fair and honourable behaviour maintained. The young Russian lieutenant Nikolaevic Tuchacevskij made use of this,

Villagers in the market of Strzałkowo, in the German-occupied part of Poland. Food and raw materials are confiscated in the occupied territories, generally without regard for the local population.

(*Opposite*) A so-called passenger dogcart in Lille, in the German-occupied part of France. Horses are confiscated in the occupied territories.

fleeing from Ingolstadt during a walk in 1917. He travelled back to Russia via Paris and became a legendary army leader of the Bolshevists, known as the 'Red Napoleon'. Before leaving Paris in 1917, he wrote a postcard to the leader of the Ingolstadt prison camp, apologizing for breaking his word of honour by fleeing.

Back at home, the population were suffering due to the ever-decreasing supply of food and clothing. The hard winter of 1916–17 in Germany, following a bad harvest, led to famine and food riots. When 'Spanish flu' then raged across the whole of Europe, more people died at home than on the front. On 11 November, the day of the German surrender, thousands of people died of the 'flu in France, including the poet Guillame Apollinaire. According to the most recent calculations, almost 50 million people died during the epidemic, most under forty years of age.

The issue of food supply in Germany and Russia was far more dramatic than in Britain and France. Agriculture provided much less produce once the men had been sent off to the front, but supplies from neutral countries were able to compensate for the shortages at least in part. The devastation of the countryside in northern and eastern France, the uncertain fate of family members behind the German front line, the deportation of sections of the population for forced labour in Germany – all of this affected French families far more than interruptions to the food supply.

Evidence of the suffering experienced during the First World War does not feature heavily in the photographs of August Fuhrmann, but reveals itself upon closer inspection. Wounded soldiers are only shown neatly bandaged in

hospital. Likewise, there are many photographs of graves – often with soliders mourning their fallen comrades – but virtually no pictures of dead bodies. When pieced together and viewed in the right context, however, Fuhrmann's images do add up to a comprehensive picture of the war and its horrors.

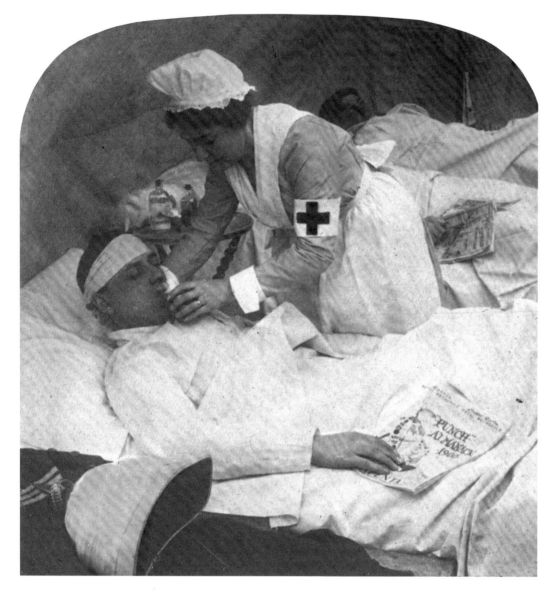

South Africa, 1901.
Before the First World War even apparently minor injuries could mean death as medical treatment often consists primarily of amputation. But by the beginning of the war medicine has made great progress. From burns to very severe head injuries, much – but not everything by a long way – can now be survived.

"We have been all day in caps and aprons at L'Evêché, marking linen and waiting for orders on the big staircase. I've also been over both hospitals. The bad cases all seem to be dropped here off the trains; there are some awful mouth, jaw, head, leg and spine cases, who can't recover, or will only be crippled wrecks. You can't realize that it has all been done on purpose, and that none of them are accidents or surgical diseases. And they seem all to take it as a matter of course; the bad ones who are conscious don't speak, and the better ones are all jolly and smiling, and ready 'to have another smack'."

Anonymous nurse on the western front

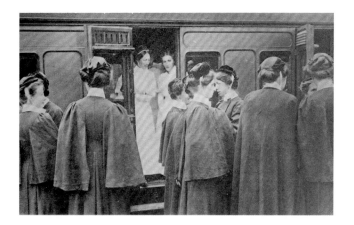

London, 1914. For Sarah Macnaughtan it is quite natural to follow the British Army to Belgium as a volunteer helper in August 1914. She is a veteran of the Red Cross – and an illustrious bevy of young, rich women go with her to the front to support the British Army in the fiercest battles of their history. But none of them could predict what awaits them in this war.

"It was one of those voyages which produce the deeply-sworn 'never again' of suffering passengers. One regretted living on an island. One was willing to vote millions for a Channel tunnel, and the only comforting verse of scripture that suggested itself for one's tombstone was 'There shall be no more sea'. One promised oneself one more voyage only, as long as life lasted, and that was back to England again. At Antwerp we were met by carriages sent for us by the British Consulate, and, feeling empty, we put on the Patent Patriotic Smile, which we believed to be suitable for 'the Front'. The Patent Patriotic Smile helped afterwards, and it was just as well to begin to practise it, even though one was still feeling very seasick."

Sarah Macnaughtan, Scottish volunteer nurse

Destroyed village, France, c. 1915. Army life at the front largely consists of waiting. Information spreads by word of mouth, and facts becomes rumours. This applies particularly to alleged war crimes by the enemy.

"I'm managing very well and we're very well fed, I haven't yet touched my supplies, keeping them for the bad days… A few days ago, those barbaric Germans, having had two Uhlans killed on patrol, the rest of the regiment occupied the two villages whose inhabitants had been guilty of shooting at them, Fléville and Affleville. They defiled the girls in front of their mothers and set fire to both villages."

Alexandre Jacqueau, French soldier

Postcard, USA, 1917. For women, service as voluntary nurses is often their only chance of going to war – and they do so with great idealism. At first they are more of a hindrance than a help to the overburdened professional nurses.

"The heroic element (a real thing among us) takes queer forms sometimes. 'No sheets, of course,' is what one hears on every side, and to eat a meal standing and with dirty hands is to 'play the game'. Maxine Elliott said, 'The nervous exhaustion attendant upon discomfort hinders work,' and she 'does herself' very well, as also do all the men of the regular forces. But volunteer corps – especially women – are heroically bent on being uncomfortable. In a way they like it, and they eat strange meals in large quantities, and feel that this is war."

Sarah Macnaughtan, Scottish volunteer nurse

Zanvoorde, Belgium, c. 1915. When firing at the enemy, the artillery cannot take religious buildings into consideration – the guns of the First World War are far too imprecise for that. The foundations of old churches are often much stronger than those of the surrounding houses, so the church walls are often the only thing that remains of a village after heavy artillery fire.

"I paid a visit recently to another wonder of the war, the Church of Vermelles. Little remains of it now, for the town has been held in succession by the Germans, French, and ourselves, and every yard of ground was lost and won a dozen times. The church is just a heap of ruins, but hanging still on one of the broken walls is a large crucifix absolutely untouched. The figure is a beautiful one, a work of art, and the face of our Lord has an expression of sadness such as I have never seen before. The whole thing may be only chance, but it is a striking sight, and cannot fail to impress one and bring home the fact that if God is scourging the world, as it well deserves, He is not indifferent to the sorrows and sufferings of His children."

Father William Doyle, chaplain with the 16th (Irish) Division

France, c. 1916. Destroyed churches near the front are converted into hospitals by the German army in occupied France.

"That I was in the meantime lying in the vaulted crypt of a ruined church that was being used as a bandaging station, and that it was Reinhard Neefe, as field chaplain, who tended to the dying close behind the front, and found me among the hopeless cases facing death, the ones no one cared about any longer, and saw to it that I was taken back to the nearest field hospital, where I was brought back to life – I only found all this out much later."

Hermann Stehr, German writer

Langemark, Belgium, c. 1915. Ruined churches come to symbolize the cruelty of the enemy and the suffering of the civilian population, especially on the Allied side. It is, however, impossible to tell which side is responsible for the destruction.

"In the cathedral, and amongst its crumbling battered aisles, a strange peace rests. The pitiful columns of the church stand here and there – the roof has long since gone. On its most sheltered side is the little graveyard, filled with crosses, where the dead lie. Here and there a shell has entered and torn a corpse from its resting-place, and bones lie scattered. On other graves a few simple flowers are laid."

Sarah Macnaughtan, Scottish volunteer nurse

◄ **Cierges, France, c. 1915.** The doctors in the field hospitals on all sides are hopelessly overworked. Under the most appalling conditions, they do everything they can to save the lives of soldiers who are often extremely seriously injured, achieving almost superhuman feats.

"Oct 5. At a Casualty Clearing Station. Shown round by CO and chief surgeon. See roomful of badly wounded having their gashes dressed under anaesthetics… 'Resurrection room', where cases, impossible to operate upon when received, are seen to by Sister and others, and wonderfully rendered capable of operation in a few days. H has done 19 big abdominal operations in a day at times of pressure. Have had 125 operations done in a day."

C.E. Montague, British war correspondent

Montmédy, France, c. 1915. Another side of modern war is represented by the countless prisoners of war – here, a group of interned French soldiers. The Hague Land War Convention of 1907 first sets out how they are to be treated – the capturing party must ensure their welfare, provide them with food, clothes and lodging, and above all treat them humanely. In the First World War these rules are soon put severely to the test on all fronts by the eight million prisoners of war.

"There were six Germans at the station today, two wounded and four prisoners. Individually I always like them, and it is useless to say I don't. They are all polite and grateful, and I thought today, when the prisoners were surrounded by a gaping crowd, that they bore themselves very well. After all, one can't expect a whole nation of mad dogs. A Scotchman said, 'The ones opposite us (ie, in the trenches) were a very respectable lot of men'."

Sarah Macnaughtan, Scottish volunteer nurse

Strzałkowo, Russian Poland, c. 1916.
The Hague Convention specifies that a state may utilize the labour of prisoners of war according to their rank and aptitude. However, prisoners may not be forced to work directly for the war effort. Rules such as these are, however, progressively ignored as the war drags on. These Russian prisoners have to build military barracks for German and Austrian soldiers.

"According to a German proverb, 'hunger is a good cook'. I dread that cook one evening when I see Russian prisoners of war outside the Neu-Ulm barracks, changing trains on their way to a new camp. They pounce on the barrels into which the cooks have thrown potato peelings and rubbish, the soldiers their leftovers, mouldy bread and bones; they reach their hands into the sour-smelling slime, they stuff that swine-fodder into their mouths."

Ernst Toller, German worker poet and soldier

Flanders, Belgium, c. 1916. For the soldiers at the front life with the dead has become an everyday normality. Often they persevere for a long time in the trenches beside dead comrades or fallen enemy soldiers. But the front line also stretches across cemeteries – and they find themselves surrounded by ruined graves.

"But what a change, what a transformation in the soul of our soldiers. At the start of the campaign, only a very few went to mass, many behaved in an uncouth manner, relieving themselves in the cemeteries adjacent to the churches and several times in the churches themselves. Today, the churches are too small to contain all the people who want to go to service. In line with orders, every soldier has his medal, and many wear a cap with a little tricolore *flag with the emblems of the Sacred Heart."*

Alexandre Jacqueau, French soldier

Somme, France, 1916. Static warfare like that of the western front never existed before the First World War. Battles last for months, they don't always have a clear beginning and almost never a real end. To evacuate the wounded, a system of ambulances is created. These must be driven to the front then driven back again – which makes the transport of soldiers and ammunition difficult. A wounded soldier, therefore, is much more valuable to the enemy than a dead one, because he puts far more of a strain on the enemy forces.

"Stretchers arrived constantly, borne by Red Cross orderlies. We were used to death and dying at our hospital, but here we met despair. Most of those lying on that straw were in extremis – nothing could be done for them. Grey ashen faces looked dully at us, they were mostly too bad to groan. It is dreadful to be impotent, to stand by grievously stricken men it is impossible to help, to see the death-sweat gathering on young faces, to have no means of easing their last moments. This is the nearest to Hell I have yet been. We put all the hopeful cases into our cars, driving one or two loads to the little station, and then returning for more, which we took back with us to Furnes."

An anonymous nurse in Belgium

Zossen, Germany, 1914. Prisoners of war in Germany – like this group of soldiers from many different countries, assembled for a propaganda photograph – generally fare better than they do in Russia. The prisoners interned in this camp in Zossen, called the 'Half-Moon Camp', were chiefly Muslim – Arabs, Africans and Indians. For them, the war is over.

"We got a feed of cheese and army biscuit in the early morning, were at Havre about four, and disembarked just before sunrise on a stormy morning with the snow beginning to fall. There were German prisoners at work on the quays. Like all the other German prisoners I've seen since they looked not sorry to be out of the hurlyburly; but it must be awful to be a prisoner – any death you can meet in war must be better, except for the hope of seeing friends again at some distant time."

C.E. Montague, British war correspondent

Montenegro, 1916.
A group of Montenegrin prisoners. Most belligerent countries adhere to the regulations of the Hague Land War Convention for the Treatment of Prisoners of War – as best they can. Prisoners are chiefly made to work in agriculture and mining, and thus become an important substitute for the men in the field. Nonetheless, with more than 2.9 million prisoners of war, Russia is hopelessly overtaxed; almost one in four of its prisoners die in captivity.

"*The Boches are being very nice this morning and letting me get on with my correspondence. My men shot two of them this morning, and I learn that the company that has the neighbouring sector has just taken four prisoners. They say they are underfed and discouraged, demoralized. Is it true? They also say that many people want to surrender, I strongly doubt that, and that they're only sending their worst men to B... des C... to punish them.*

  It's true that we aren't giving them a holiday in these enchanting woods. But I'm still suspicious of their gossip, in my sector at any rate, no prisoners, we're too close and we're only negotiating with rifle bullets."

Alexandre Jacqueau, French soldier

Neidenburg, Germany, 1916. Wounded German soldiers in a hospital. One of the soldiers' greatest fears is gas gangrene. Even a small wound can become inflamed if contaminated and can within a few days, sometimes only hours, prove fatal. Even today, a quick amputation is often the only way of saving the patient's life.

"Sunday, September 20th. Began with early service at the Jesuit School Hospital at 6.30, and the rest of the day one will never forget. Three trains full of wounded, numbering altogether 1,175 cases, have been dressed at the station to-day; we were sent down at 11 this morning. You boarded a cattle-truck, armed with a tray of dressings and a pail; the men were lying on straw; had been in trains for several days; most had only been dressed once, and many were gangrenous. If you found one urgently needed amputation or operation, or was likely to die, you called an MO to have him taken off the train for hospital. No one grumbled or made any fuss."

Anonymous nurse on the western front

Przemyśl, Galicia, 1916. Galician Jews on the way to synagogue. The immeasurable suffering of the Jews in the Second World War often leads us to forget that the Jewish diaspora, which lives across the whole of Eastern Europe, is already the target of hatred and pogroms in the First World War.

"The Jewish pogrom has been underway since yesterday evening. The Cossacks waited until the Jews set off to the synagogue for their prayers before setting upon them with whips. They were deaf to any pleas for mercy, regardless of age... What were they going to do with them?"

Helena Jabłońska, Polish widow under siege in Przemyśl

Comines, Franco-Belgian border, c. 1916. In most cases the soldiers fighting at the front don't share the hatred stoked by propaganda at home. In man-to-man combat, no mercy is shown to the enemy. But if the situation permits, fallen soldiers – friend or foe – are given a decent burial, like this English officer being carried to the grave by German soldiers.

▶ **Janów, Russia, 1914.** In January 1918, the Spanish flu breaks out across the world. Normal influenza affects mainly the young, the old and those with weak immune systems. But this epidemic mostly carries off healthy adults. Between 50 and 100 million people die worldwide. Even today it is not clear where the epidemic comes from. The flu is called 'Spanish' because the outbreak was reported only in neutral Spain's press; reporting was censored in the belligerent countries.

"On 13.7.1918 reports came in from the front that some of the crews had fallen violently ill with flu. Order: everything stays in the trenches where possible!
Flu, influenza, catarrhal fever, highly infectious disease normally appearing in epidemic form, caused by the influenza bacteria. (Der Kleine Brockhaus, 1915)"

Edlef Köppen, German soldier

"I have been out all day visiting cemeteries and isolated graves along half our front. There was a Frenchwoman with some white flowers to put on the grave of her son. While she was arranging them on the grave there came into the cemetery one of the usual little processions – an English sergeant leading, then the chaplain, then a dead soldier, on a stretcher, with a Union Jack over him, and half a dozen privates walking behind. They passed close by the woman, and when they were just past her she gathered up half her flowers and fell in behind them. When they came to the grave and the chaplain began to read the burial service, she knelt down on the ground near them and stayed like that, praying, till the service was over, and then came forward, evidently overcoming her shyness with an effort, and dropped the flowers on the man in the grave, and then went away, weeping. I think I have hardly ever seen anything so touching."

C.E. Montague, British war correspondent

"I don't go to the station so often to help in the Red Cross booth. Grandmother has organized so many helpers that it's better if I do my schoolwork or help with the housework in my free time, for example mending or darning mountains of laundry. I hate sewing and darning. If I only knew what I'm supposed to wear for dance class, I hardly have a single good dress left. My school uniform is one of Willi's old sailor blouses, and a pleated skirt made of one of mother's old dresses, but the skirt is in pretty bad shape already."

Elfriede Kuhr, German schoolgirl

Serbia, c. 1916. The First World War was sparked by the murder of Archduke Franz Ferdinand by Serbian extremists. The primary aim of the Austro-Hungarian army – which initially suffered heavy defeats – is the conquest and destruction of Serbia. Serbian prisoners of war, such as those in this column, are often court-martialled and executed.

"My nearest neighbour was a German woman, her husband was Hungarian. They were kindly simple souls whose hearts had been wrung by the tragedies played beneath their eyes. They had seen the neighbours, with whom they had lived in friendly intercourse, brutally ill-treated and killed, they had seen Serbian soldiers marched through by their captors, those falling out through fatigue or illness being bayoneted and left, huddled bleeding heaps by the roadside, silent witnesses to Kultured methods of depraved barbarity."

Dr Caroline Matthews, Scottish doctor in Serbia

Frankfurt, Germany, c. 1916. In the course of the war over two million Entente soldiers are made prisoners of war by the Germans. There had been no plans to take care of so many prisoners.

Italy, c. 1917. For most prisoners, like these Italian soldiers, the war is over as soon as they are taken captive. The longer the fighting and dying goes on, the higher the number of those who give themselves up voluntarily just to escape the horror of the front.

"Where are we supposed to put all these prisoners! We now see so many prisoner transports coming through our station, that the long brown coats and matted hair are no longer a novelty. Fräulein Gumprecht, who came for coffee today, said the prisoners were just going to bring famine and plagues into the country. 'Why don't they just shoot them?' she shouted. Well, we thought it was a terrible idea, shooting the prisoners on top of everything else that has been happening."

Elfriede Kuhr, German schoolgirl

"But there are hardships in Serbia for prisoners of war which are difficult to realize in England. Serbia was war-stained, a little nation just awakening from a fiendish grip which would have throttled the spirit of a less hardy people. Many of the prisoners, both officers and men, told me that they had never fired a shot. The moral? Men who are made to serve beneath the strong hand of an alien can be forced into the ranks but their hearts are their own and when no spontaneous call of duty has stirred them to the effort they are better left at home."

Dr Caroline Matthews, Scottish doctor in Serbia

Belgium, c. 1916. The stalemate of the trenches bears strange blossoms. While solders who dare to venture into no-man's-land are immediately shot by enemy snipers, stretcher-bearers can cross the death zone unharmed, to recover the dead and the wounded.

Krosnowice, Russian Poland, 1915. Events on the eastern front are considerably more variable than in the west. Towns are conquered and reconquered, the front shifts again and again, particularly in the territory of contemporary Poland. The many little villages and towns are not a match for the troops attacking and marching through them.

"Curiously quiet morning after the slaughter. As if it were perfectly natural, only about two hundred metres away from me, tall, sinewy Canadian orderlies in coats and steel helmets, burying their dead on the spot. They've planted a big Red Cross flag in the ground beside them. Not a shot is fired. Again and again the Canadians carry the wounded over their shoulders to the graves. Our stretcher-bearers scour the field as well. Jakob Lorenzen, Hannes Meier, Müller, Julius Bendixen and two others whom we'd already missed were found, all felled by a shell. They were buried in a shell-hole."

Gerrit Engelke, German worker poet and soldier

"In the dark and quiet all the countless joints and wheels of the vast organism were still mysteriously turning. Once, in a cloud of dust, we passed troops marching toward the front – tired faces, laughing faces – the shout 'Man in the road!' and then the glimpse of a couple of Red Cross men kneeling by a soldier who had given out on the way; once, in the black pines, cows driven by two little frightened peasant children; once a long line of bearded Jews, bound, with packs on their backs, for what was left of their homes; a supply-train, a clanking battery, and now and then other motors like ours with shrouded grey figures, streaking by in a flashing mist of dust."

Arthur Ruhl, American journalist

Für's Vaterland

Postcard, Germany, during the war. In propaganda – such as this German postcard – death in the field is stylized as a heroic sacrifice that contributes to the final victory. For those at home, however, there is no greater horror than the letter from the commander of the father, brother or son's unit announcing this 'heroic death'.

"Dear Frau Krein
By the time you read these lines, you will already have received the news of the heroic death of your dear husband.

Your pain over the loss of this loyal husband and father is great and justified. For almost two months your husband belonged to my platoon. He was a good and dutiful soldier, and because of these qualities he was both dear and precious to me and to his other superiors. Thus he remained a hero for the first sacred cause of our fatherland, and a spark of pride can mingle with your justified grief, admittedly small consolation! But your husband's blood will not have flowed in vain. If Germany, as we rightly hope, soon meets its blessed time, you have given your best for it. Honour the brave war hero in his early war grave.

For reasons of duty it was unfortunately impossible for me to give him the last rites this morning. May the Lord God comfort you and yours in your great pain."

Nimtsch, Reserve Lieutenant

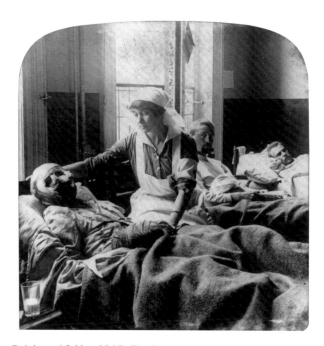

Belgium, 18 May 1915. The first proven gas attack in the First World War is in August 1914, when French troops deploy tear-gas grenades against the Germans. The first deployment of deadly gas is carried out by German troops on 22 April 1915.

"The Canadians and English who poured in from Ypres were terribly damaged, and the asphyxiating gas seems to have been simply diabolical. It was awful to see human beings so mangled, and I never get one bit accustomed to it. God! how they were knocked about! The vast rooms echoed to the cries of pain. The men were vowing they could never face shells and hand grenades any more. They were so newly wounded, poor boys; but they come up smiling when their country calls again. But it isn't right. This damage to human life is horrible. It is madness to slaughter these thousands of young men. Almost at last, in a rage, one feels inclined to cry out against the sheer imbecility of it. Why bring lives into the world and shell them out of it with jagged pieces of iron, and knives thrust through their quivering flesh? The pain of it is all too much. I am sick with seeing suffering."

Sarah Macnaughtan, Scottish nurse in Ypres

Austria, 1916. From the start of the war, the Austro-Hungarian army is hopelessly overtaxed in logistical terms. Its own soldiers have barely enough to eat, which makes it all the more difficult to feed prisoners of war.

"Then the prisoners were marshalled. Then twelve of us were chosen, one of them me, to take them to headquarters. We marched from the morning until one o'clock in the morning. We had all our equipment, 40 kg, on an empty stomach. We took frequent rests, and the Russians had already begged my reserve rusks off me. They had bacon with them and black bread. They gave me some of it and allayed my hunger. After the handover at night we got black coffee, and were glad to have something hot."

Karl Kasser, Austrian soldier

Postcard, Japan, c. 1915. Japan's role in the war – apart from the conquest of the German colony of Tsingtao in China – was restricted to sending nurses to the western front.

"There was our Red Cross envoys' concern about giving their best, and at the same time there was the naked aristocratic curiosity of the French volunteer nurses. East and West, pragmatism and exoticism simultaneously."

Tōson Shimazaki, Japanese author in Paris

◀ **Carpathians, Austria-Hungary, c. 1916.** The longer the war lasts, the harder the work and the worse the conditions for the prisoners of war. Here Russian prisoners of war are working in a quarry in the Carpathians.

"I took my first trip to the shaft with a Russian, as we first had to learn. At two o'clock in the afternoon our team went down and had to work until ten at night. The Russian and I climbed down a ladder into the depths. The tunnel was sixty metres deep. At first you get dizzy. The other tunnels were even deeper, up to six hundred metres. Now we worked for an hour; the Russian, together with the other prisoners, broke up the coal and I had to drive it away on a trolley. On the second day we went down with the others. That was better. Had to fetch coal on the trolley. The work was dirty, but you got used to it."

Karl Kasser, Austrian prisoner of war in Siberia

Postcard, USA, 1918. Rumours spread extremely quickly, both at the front and at home. Propaganda picks up the rumours and – as with this postcard – uses them to its own advantage.

"Some terrible stories of the war are coming through from the front. An officer told us that when they take a trench, the only thing which describes what the place is like is strawberry jam. Another said that in one trench the sides were falling, and the Germans used corpses to make a wall, and kept them in with piles fixed into the ground. Hundreds of men remain unburied."

Sarah Macnaughtan, Scottish volunteer nurse

Rubnow, Russian Poland, 1915. Even today there are no reliable figures about how many children are orphaned by the First World War. It is known that in all front-line territories religious communities set up orphanages to look after the children.

"There was a certain bazaar at Dunkerque, a big departmental store of cheap goods, which was a perfect fairyland of toys and Christmas presents. Now, my friend and I were deeply interested in a little orphanage near us at Furnes, where twenty war-orphans, boys from three to fifteen years old, were cared for by nuns. So we went to the bazaar and bought things that boys like, also presents for our friends. Then the doctor who drove us in, took us to a hotel dinner. All these seem ordinary events, but to us they were delightful excitements after having lived in a kitchen and eaten bully beef for months. We were like girls from boarding-school let out for a holiday!"

Anonymous nurse in France

USA, 1917. As the war continues, volunteer and professional nurses are forged into an inseparable unit. Long before the USA enters the war, many American volunteers come to Europe to help the wounded.

St Petersburg, c. 1915. The wives and daughters of the ruling houses of Europe set the best examples. Many – such as Grand Duchess Tatiana, the daughter of Tsar Nicholas II, shown here – help as volunteer nurses in hospitals at the front.

"God help us, what a mixture it all is! Here were men talking of the very sound of bayonets on human flesh; here were men not only asphyxiated by gas, but blinded by the pepper that the Germans mix with it; and here were men determined to give no quarter – yet they were babbling of Loch Lomond's side and their mothers, and fighting as to who should give up their beds to each other."

Sarah Macnaughtan, Scottish volunteer nurse

"Oh, how dull, empty and cold it is here. I'd like so much to go back to our warm and sunny Sevastopol. The sun is shining the whole day but it doesn't make us warm. We all went to the hospital church today for the liturgy. Then we spent some time with the wounded in the hospital. There were only two dressings, I even felt ashamed that there were so few of them. In the afternoon Mother and all of us went to her Uhlan hospital where all the regiment ladies were present."

Grand Duchess Tatiana, daughter of Tsar Nicholas II

Saalburg camp, Germany, c. 1915. Plagues like cholera and typhus kill more people during the First World War than all the hostilities put together. Hygiene conditions in the barracks are often poor, and latrines are not dug far enough away from water sources – an ideal breeding-ground for diseases.

"One bowl contained boiled sauerkraut, boiled potato peelings, and gave out a perfectly revolting smell. Stirring this mess round with a listless forefinger, I discovered that potato sprouts were clinging to the peelings, but these had been boiled away into the likeness of grey worms, while the peelings themselves were crusted with dirt. The only thing you could say for this supper was that it was thoroughly cooked. The other bowl, as I had guessed, contained drinking water; though it might possibly have been washing water. In any case it was so rank with the smell of kerosene that it was scarcely suited for either purpose."

Marina Yurlova, Russian Cossack soldier

The Hague, Netherlands, before the war. When Antwerp in Belgium is conquered by the Germans on 10 August 1914, almost a million people flee from Belgium to the neutral Netherlands. The Dutch are completely overwhelmed and don't know how to accommodate all these people, let alone feed them.

"What I did not foresee, however, was the mass of people that has flooded into our country, causing our strategy to collapse. The Dutch government did not foresee this, nor the Belgian government – nobody did. Lack of space; over-population because, motivated by profit, some private persons took in six or seven refugees, for whom they received 0.35 guilders per adult and 0.20 guilders per child; unhygienic conditions, and the outbreak of infectious diseases."

Cort van der Linden, Dutch Prime Minister

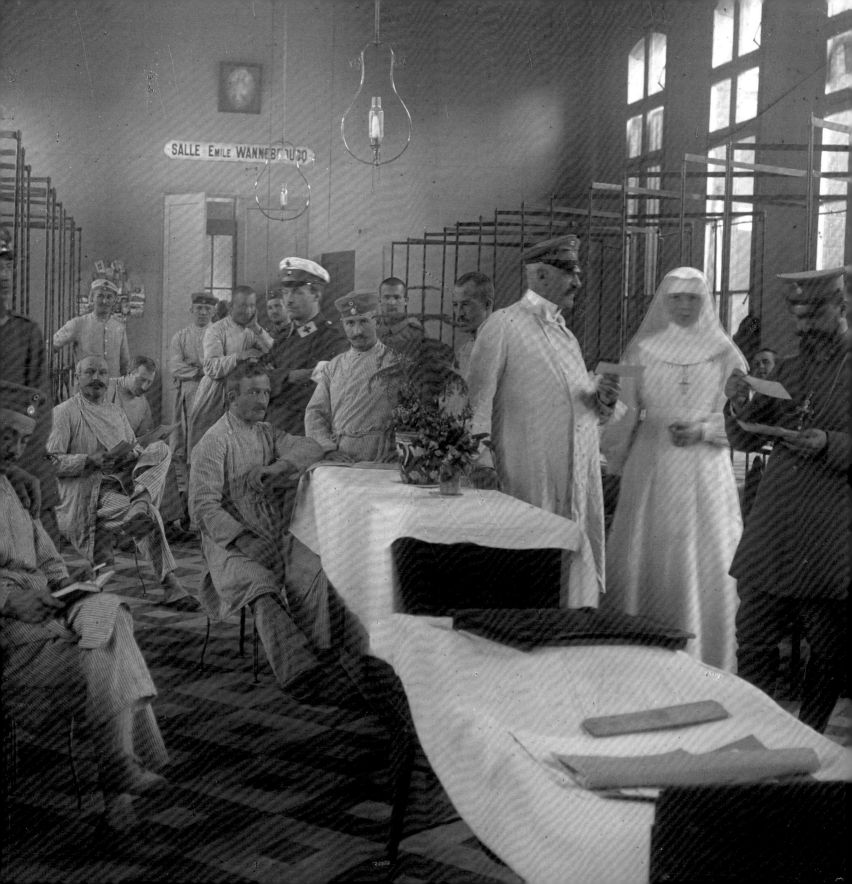

◄ **Lille, France, c. 1916.** The paradox of medical treatment in the First World War is that the aim is not to heal wounded soldiers. Its sole purpose is to make them fit for battle again as quickly as possible, so that they can go back to the front.

"While the Battle of the Yser was proceeding every nerve was strained day and night to cope with the work. Then after two or three weeks things died down to a few casualties each day. During that time we assumed more the nature of a base hospital, and instead of packing off all who could travel next morning in ambulances, we nursed them to something approaching convalescence, or till another rush came. We had permanently attached to us two Belgian colonels, a major and some lieutenants who examined the wounded each morning, placing tickets over the beds of those who were to be moved to France and England."

An anonymous nurse in Belgium

Belgium, 1917. As a volunteer nurse in a British ambulance unit like this one, Sarah Macnaughtan experienced the full horror of the western front in Belgium, but the war in the Russian Caucasus will prove even more of an ordeal.

"It was towards the beginning of fall, when the term ended, when they talked of getting jobs for us, five or six of us being assigned at a time to whatever positions fell vacant; and it was almost winter before I left Tiflis for Erivan, where I was to join the Red Cross. When we passed through the streets, as the winter grew older, we used to be assaulted by desperate bands of children, more than half naked, their bellies swollen out of all proportion, their legs so thin that you wondered how they could stand upright on them, their lean ribs almost tearing through the stretched skin."

Sarah Macnaughtan, Scottish volunteer nurse

HOME

"I wander through the early spring of the English Garden, snowdrops are blossoming, crocuses, the first violets… young women sit in bright clothes, children sing, music plays, people are happy. I want to forget the war. But I can't."

Ernst Toller, German soldier, dismissed from the force as unfit to fight after being wounded

On 31 July 1914, just two days before the outbreak of war, Kaiser Wilhelm pronounced a state of siege in Germany. Executive authority passed over to the commanders of military districts and fortresses. That did not mean, however, that military officers were now commanding in the towns and villages. The military had neither the necessary personnel nor the knowledge for that. The mid- and lower-level bureaucracy continued working, and nothing much changed in administrative life.

In France, a state of siege was announced on 2 August, followed the next day by the declaration that the country was at war. The consequences were graver than in Germany. The French military seized powers from the police and mayors, while military courts made arbitrary judgements. French historian Jean-Jacques Becker explains: 'This gradually led to a genuine dictatorship of the High Command.'

The railway bridge near Wassen in Switzerland. Both France and Germany had plans to attack Switzerland, although these were never put into effect.

This came to an end only in 1916, when the image of the military had been so damaged by its many failures that management and jurisdiction could be normalized again.

At the beginning of the war, many citizens believed that they had to defend the land on the home front. Nuns in both Protestant Berlin and Catholic Münster were imprisoned on suspicion of being Russian spies. The 'Cars of Gold' hysteria which broke out in Germany and Austria-Hungary at the start of the war had dire consequences. Hearing rumours that cars filled with gold were en route from France and Belgium to Russia, armed citizens forcibly stopped cars and searched them. It cost many lives, particularly when officers and high officials were reluctant to stop their cars. The ruling powers then stepped in, suppressing the gold hunt and, with it, the persecution of foreigners.

This was one of the reasons why Germany did not see attacks on foreigners of the kind which took place in Russia, France, Britain and, later, the United States. Workers and tradesmen who had emigrated from Germany to Britain became the

A family in Romania, before the war. Romania is drawn into the war by territorial promises on behalf of the Entente – and suffers a complete defeat against the Central Powers.

target of public suspicion. Basil Thomson, director of the Special Branch of counterintelligence, spoke of an 'espionage virus' which had infected all strata of society. The police in London received more than 400 reports a day, with the result that investigations ground to a halt. When the *Daily Mail* proclaimed 'Lock Up All the Germans, Confiscate Their Property' on its front page, numerous shops were destroyed.

There were very few Germans in France. One of the few spectacular cases was the ousting of German exhibitors from the *Exposition Internationale* in Lyon. The right-wing extremist *Action Française* found no better victim for its campaign against foreign enemies than the Swiss food product company Maggi. Before the war, Maggi had sold more than 60 million litres of pasteurized milk, which were now declared to have been poisoned. Maggi branches were vandalized as a result.

A stretch of railway track in Germany, before the war. The railway allows the belligerent nations in the First World War to assemble in their millions on various fronts quicker than ever before.

Everyday life was soon defined by less spectacular matters. The most important was the production of arms. The quantities of ammunition being fired on the fronts would have been unimaginable before the war. At the start of the war, so many young men signed up that measures needed to be found to keep up production levels for arms and armaments. In Britain and Germany, skilled workers were exempt from service. In France they were drafted but then forced back into the factories. In Russia only two per cent of workers were released to go to the front.

In the midst of war, social peace was most affected by the rising prices and insufficient food supply. In Russia, the ample harvests in the Ukraine didn't make it to the towns in the north due to a lack of transport capacities. When more and more men from farming families were forced to go to the front, it led to revolts in the European and Asian regions. Together with the assertive and increasingly unsatisfied workers of the huge armament industries in Petrograd, a revolutionary potential built up which contributed to the fall of the Tsarist regime in 1917.

In Germany, the most severe consequences of the food shortage can be traced back to the British naval blockade. Although only very few essential food goods had been transported via the North Sea ports before the war (and the fact that even during the war some deliveries from Scandinavia arrived via the German marine-controlled Baltic Sea) the supply of fertilizer and fuel was so greatly affected that the food supply chain increasingly broke down as time passed.

In the autumn of 1916, Romania was occupied by the Central Powers and two million tonnes of grain, hundreds of thousands of livestock and a million tonnes of crude oil were seized. But the transport capacities weren't enough to get the loot to Germany. There, the winter of 1916–17 was one of bitter starvation, with riotous scenes in front of the empty bakeries and greengrocers.

The willingness to suffer for the war reduced as perceptibly in Germany as it did in Russia. Rising prices led to panic buying and profiteering. Creative entrepreneurs even made good business by setting up wooden figures of Hindenburg and getting citizens to pay to hammer in nails. The 'Iron Hindenburg' in front of the Berlin Reichstag was twelve metres high, weighed 26 tonnes and brought in significant proceeds. But none of that could be found when the company in charge, 'Luftfahrerdank GmbH', went bankrupt after completing the work.

The French never suffered starvation like the Germans did. But the prices increased steadily, after having remained stable for more than a hundred years. This made *'la vie chère'* seem all the more

A market in Morocco, before the war. Tensions over Germany's territorial ambitions here had almost led to a European war in 1911. During the First World War, German settlers in Morocco were interned by the French.

shocking. The reason was that, just as in Germany, the government was wary of increasing taxes. Instead, loans were taken and bank notes printed. Everything was fine until 1916 when inflation set in, followed shortly after by a wave of strikes. They ended when companies gave in to pressure from the government and increased salaries. Unlike in Germany or Russia, the social clashes did not lead to any influential pacifist tendencies. Even left-wing radical syndicalists had no doubt that the country had to be defended against German invasion. The *'Union sacrée'*, announced in 1914, managed to survive the crisis of 1917.

In Britain, it was far from certain that the majority of the population would be in favour of war. Supporters of the Labour Party, as well as Conservative and Liberal voters, all wanted peace. But reports of the violent acts of the German military against 'poor little Belgium' turned the mood. The opinion that Britain had to fight 'on the side of right and honour' was now almost unanimous. That even applied in Ireland, where the independence movement

against British rule was in opposition. The anti-German sentiment won out, even though the German government spared no cost in attempting to corrupt leaders of the Irish nationalists. They succeeded only with Sir Roger Casement, but he had no support from his countrymen and was hanged as a traitor to his country in 1916.

Even while the war was still going on, the term 'total war' began to be used in France. This was intended to express that the 'industrial war' required sacrifice from the home front in order to supply the actual front with weapons, ammunition, barbed wire, gas and gas masks, telephones and radios, cars and airplanes. When inflation led to strikes, this was consequently referred to as being a 'stab in the back' for the fighting soldiers. This happened first not in Germany, but in Britain.

'Total war' also meant that the people at home were risking their lives just as much as soldiers on the front. Everywhere, civilians were being killed in air raids: in Germany as well as in Belgium, France and Britain. The bomb attacks which the Austrian secret service unleashed in Italy with support from Catholic and Socialist anti-war protestors were also deadly. Those involved in planning the acts of sabotage were alleged to include Rudolf von Gerlach, the private secretary of Pope Benedict XV, and lawyer Giuseppe Ambrogetti, another close confidant of the pope's.

There were no sympathies for anti-war protestors in Germany either. But there, fewer and fewer people believed in defensive warfare by 1918. Inflation, famine and fear of another cold winter led to a steady increase in the number of Germans who had had enough of the 'state of siege' and wanted peace. When, in the summer of 1918, the ruling powers finally wanted to negotiate peace in the face of their military defeats, it was too late.

Austro-Hungarian representatives of the press at army headquarters. It is only through the press that the population at home learns of events at the front – and those reports are of course heavily censored.

(*Opposite*) A village in the Dolomites, fought over between Italy and Austro-Hungary. Austrians and Italians are at home on both sides of the front. Which country they fight for is decided not by their conviction but by their place of residence.

During the war, Fuhrmann dedicates almost all of his efforts to photographing the war itself. New images of life at home are rarely published. In order to illuminate the experience of life at home attention must, therefore, be turned to the series of photographs which emerged just before the war – particularly when looking at life in the Allied countries, where Fuhrmann was unable to photograph after the outbreak of hostilities.

Pinzola, South Tyrol, before the war. Home front and trenches – these are two different worlds in which the wives and husbands of the First World War find themselves. Life at home is soon just as unimaginable for the soldiers as the trenches are for the families who stay at home.

"Went for a walk alone through the forest this morning. The weather was so glorious. Now I can understand you very well when you, my dear Robert, walk alone into the forest. On the one hand the mountains were white with snow, because the sun doesn't quite come through, and on the other side the forest was in bright sunlight. Before I went into the forest I saw a sergeant standing at our kitchen window with the cook. I said as a joke that that wasn't allowed. He said, 'Shooting people dead for three years isn't allowed either.'"

Anna Pöhland, wife of a German soldier

Montenegro, 1916.
Montenegrin children greet occupying soldiers. For children especially, life during the occupation is often very difficult. They cannot yet understand that one wrong word can mean death for their family.

"That afternoon some more officers came in telling me they would like black coffee. One was a typical Prussian – big, red, and brutal. He tried to talk to the children. They would have nothing to do with him. He walked about the room twirling his riding whip, laughing, and satisfied with the result of the battle. So great was his satisfaction he must even express it to the children. 'Russky kaput!' (the Russians are finished!) he kept saying over and over.

Wladek could at last stand it no longer. He went right up to the officer with his brother and sister by the hand, saying, 'Nein, nein—German kaput!' I caught the boy, begging him to be quiet. The officer shook his riding whip over us. 'We see how you teach your children, Madame! You must make the boy say, "Russky kaput", or I will beat him till he does!'"

Laura de Gozdawa Turczynowicz, American woman living in occupied Russian Poland

German postcard, c. 1915. Although in the First World War artillery, gas and machine-gun fire have long since eradicated the archetypal war hero, propaganda needs brave warriors who can be revered. In the First World War these are most often the pilots.

"Our planes have fired on Harwich, Dover and Calais. Yesterday there was a big air raid on the Russian military port of Reval. In our stationery shops they are selling postcards with photographs of our most famous pilot heroes. Every time I have saved twenty pfennigs I buy a postcard of a pilot. I want to fill a whole album of them; that will be interesting later on. Next to lots of photographs I've already had to paint a cross, signifying death."

Elfriede Kuhr, German schoolgirl

Kiel, Germany, before the war. Germany is a frontrunner in the delivery of post. A total of 28 billion postcards are delivered in the course of the war, along with letters and packages. In the big cities the postman comes up to eleven times a day. So worries are quick to spread if a husband at the front is unable to write for a few days in the field.

"My dear, unfortunate husband!
You can't imagine what terrible thoughts and mental torture I have had this week. We weren't used to you not writing. We thought you'd already gone into the field. I saw you in battle in the dream. It was terrible."

Anna Pöhland, wife of a German soldier

Salo, Italy, before the war. Although the war rages hundreds, or even thousands, of kilometres from the home front, it still occupies almost all of the lives of those who remain at home.

"The offensive against Italy is all that we have been thinking about for the last few days. It has gone with the usual great rush. If only our troops can come in time to stop it! I have to be cheerful and make myself more optimistic than I really am, and quote the Marne, and so on, for Mrs Jaeger is in the depths of despair, and to hear her one would think the whole war were lost."

Ethel Cooper, Australian piano teacher living in Leipzig

Scutari, Istanbul, before the war. About 3,000 British and French citizens are living in Istanbul at the outbreak of war. Most have never been to England or any other European country. When the Entente powers begin shelling the Gallipoli peninsula, the Ottoman government proposes to send them to exposed positions on the front line – as targets for the Allied fleet.

"Naturally my first question when I received this startling information was whether the warships were really bombarding defenceless towns. If they were murdering non-combatant men, women, and children in this reckless fashion, such an act of reprisal as Enver now proposed would probably have had some justification. I soon discovered, indeed, that the Allied fleet was not bombarding Moslem villages at all. The British navy was not violating the rules of civilized warfare, for Gallipoli had long since been evacuated of its civilian population, and the Turks had established military headquarters in several of the houses, which had properly become the object of the Allied attack. I certainly knew of no rule of warfare which prohibited an attack upon a military headquarters. As to the stories of murdered civilians, men, women, and children, these proved to be gross exaggerations, as almost the entire civilian population had long since left; any casualties resulting from the bombardment must have been confined to the armed forces of the empire."

Henry Morgenthau Sr, American ambassador to the Ottoman Empire from 1913 to 1918

Falkenstein, Austria-Hungary, before the war. Before the war Europe was almost more open to the world than it is today; it was possible to travel from one end of the continent to the other without passport or visa. Banks flourished in every country, but wartime changes the economy too. Austria-Hungary, whose economy is seriously damaged by the war, forbids the private ownership of foreign currency, to prevent the outflow of capital.

"*Some farmers living on the outskirts of Vienna, whose families have been professionally attended by my husband, had already during my husband's lifetime wanted to prove their affection and gratitude by little presents of foodstuffs. My husband had flatly refused these tokens of appreciation. I now resolved to visit these people. Liesbeth was coughing a great deal, and in her condition nourishing food was a vital necessity. I drew from my bank 20,000 kronen (about £833) in cash. The bank clerk, who had attended to me and advised me for years, recommended me to convert my money into Swiss francs. When I objected that private dealings in foreign currencies were not allowed, he whispered to me that he would manage it for me if I would authorize him to do so. The transaction must, of course, be effected secretly, since it was forbidden by law. I had already resolved that day to infringe one law by the illicit purchase of supplies, but now I nervously rejected my adviser's offer. 'You will regret it, gnädige Frau. Only Switzerland and Holland will keep their currencies stable.'*"

Anna Eisenmenger, Austrian middle-class woman in Vienna

Flensburg, Germany, before the war. As the war drags on, food supplies become tight in Germany and Austria-Hungary. There are two main reasons for this: first, the workforce of millions of men, now at the front, can not be completely replaced, and second, these countries were dependent on imported raw materials, and these are now unable to get through because of the British naval blockade. The black market in food booms.

"I have a visitor here in the shape of Frau Lewicka again. She came this afternoon, laden up to the eyes with eatables. I could not believe my senses and then discovered, to my mixed horror and amusement, that she is making a small private business out of buying food in Poland, getting it smuggled in and selling it in Berlin at very considerable profit. Beaming with pride she unpacked ten dozen eggs, pounds of bacon, dried peas, dried beans and lard, and said that I was to have anything I want at cost price, but other people were to pay Berlin prices!"

Ethel Cooper, Australian piano teacher living in Germany

Bonn, Germany, before the war. Millions of war-weary soldiers are dismissed from the army on grounds of injury and have to find their way back into civilian life in their home towns. They have escaped the hell of war – but at home there is no system of social security to catch them.

"I wander through the early spring of the English Garden, snowdrops are blossoming, crocuses, the first violets, on the trees the young buds sprout with the rising sap, the light green velvet of the wide expanses of lawn shines tenderly, in front of the Japanese pavilion young women sit in bright clothes, children sing, music plays, people are happy. I want to forget the war. But I can't. For four weeks, six weeks I manage, then suddenly it assails me again, I meet it everywhere, in front of the altar by Matthias Grünewald I see, through the painting, the witches' cauldron in the Priesterwald, my shredded, wounded comrades, cripples appear in my way, black-veiled, grief-stricken women. Oh, flight was in vain."

Ernst Toller, German soldier, dismissed from the force as unfit to fight after being wounded

Village of Kreuzberg, Germany, before the war. The soldiers living at the front yearn for home – and for their families. Their children grow up without a father.

"We have such warm days now that the children run around as if it were high summer. For our little ones I had to make their summer dresses longer. On Sunday I'll make them some new ones, from the flowery fabric that was in their four-poster beds. Only a shame that you, dear Robert, can't be here to see how the children are growing up."

Anna Pöhland, wife of a German soldier, in a letter to her husband at the front

Montenegro, before the war. Even before the war begins, the first streams of refugees start moving from the border areas of Germany, France, Austria-Hungary, Belgium and Russia. It is often the old and weak who flee from the approaching armies. It is a flight into the unknown.

"Wherever one goes, in every quarter and at every hour, among the busy, strongly stepping Parisians one sees these other people, dazed and slowly moving – men and women with sordid bundles on their backs… children dragging at their hands… the great army of refugees. Their faces are unmistakable and unforgettable… here they are, in a strange country, among unfamiliar faces and new ways, with nothing left to them in the world but the memory of burning homes and massacred children and young men dragged to slavery…"

Edith Wharton, American novelist living in France

East Prussia, 1915. A school building destroyed by Russian troops. The closer the front comes, the more rash are people's attempts to escape the war, particularly on the eastern front, where several big 'fortress towns' are about to be besieged by the advancing Russians.

"This morning the gendarmerie and the police were sent out and ordered everyone to pack up immediately, with barely time to throw some clothes into a bundle… they even dragged the sick out of the beds… the horror! Children are separated from their families. Everyone has become heartless. A mother with two children boarded the train and her three-year-old child was left behind when it moved off. She wanted to jump off, but it was too late."

Helena Jabłońska, Polish widow under siege in Przemyśl

The Austrian Alps, before the war. After the outbreak of war, and alongside the stream of everyday field post, millions of ominous letters and postcards were sent – reports to families about the injury or even death of their loved ones.

"*Today a letter arrived signed by Erni but written in an unfamiliar hand. Erni is lying wounded at Innsbruck. His life is in no danger. An injury to the eyes, which they hope is not serious. As soon as he is fit to be moved he will come to Vienna. 'An injury to the eyes, which they hope is not serious.' I felt a vague, terrible anxiety for Erni's big, blue, childlike eyes. Liesbeth soothed me. We persuaded ourselves that we ought to be glad and grateful when a slight wound brought our men into a hospital and so, for the time being, into safety. 'How glad I was,' said Liesbeth, 'when Rudi came to Vienna with his arm wound. And now we shall soon have Erni here and be able to nurse and spoil him.' A Surgeon-Major-General, who is a friend of ours, has promised me to expedite Erni's transference to Vienna, so I have given up for the time being my plan of going to Innsbruck.*"

Anna Eisenmenger, Austrian middle-class woman in Vienna

"Gretel and I are playing a new game, as I no longer join in with the boys' war games. I pulled the green garden table from the bower into the middle of Aunt Otter's garden, put the two green benches on top of each other and set them up on the table. That's my plane, a Fokker double decker. Its name is 'Flea'. I adapted one wheel from Gretel's old doll's pram into a propeller, another as my steering wheel. An old rootstalk is my machine gun, with which I can shoot through the rotating propeller. That's what real fighter pilots do. As 'Lieutenant von Yellenic' I sit between the two wobbly benches on the table, and then it gets going. Gretel stands below as 'Sister Martha' and waves."

Elfriede Kuhr, German schoolgirl

Lohr, Germany, before the war. In the later winters of the war, Germany lacks not only food but also fuel, especially coal. Many collieries have lost their miners to the army. The mining of coal in the First World War was barely mechanized, but depended on the efficiency of the coal miners.

"*From Bayreuth we are told: the coal shortage is making itself felt even in Villa Wahnfried. Frau Cosima Wagner, who incidentally delights in astonishing sprightliness, and whom one can see taking her daily walks even in terrible weather, is celebrating her eightieth birthday on the second day of the Christmas holidays. In the last issue of the* Oberfränkische Zeitung, *Siegfried Wagner is now publishing the following request: 'Because of a lack of coal the reception rooms in Wahnfried cannot be heated, we must to our intense regret ask the friends of our house kindly to abstain from wishing our mother personal best wishes for her eightieth birthday. Siegfried Wagner and family.'*"

From the diary of Edlef Köppen

◄ **Shipyard workers in the port of Kiel, Germany, before the war.** Due to the British naval blockade, German ports receive fewer resources as the war goes on. The result is that from 25 January 1915, food is rationed in Germany; that is, officially one can at first buy bread, later also eggs, butter, milk and other foods, only with the appropriate food card. In 1916 cards are even introduced for the purchase of clothes and shoes.

"You will probably have read in the newspaper about the sale of bones and spare ribs at Borcher's, that is issued by the military authorities. As the crush on Osterstrasse was impossible, they now started selling at the slaughterhouse. You can't believe how many women and children were standing there. I wanted something too, but when I'd been standing there for one hour, they said the cards we needed to redeem had been used up. Well, we and some of our female comrades were prepared to demonstrate. We went over to the women and said we were going to go to the food commission. About a quarter of an hour later we had several hundred women who were willing to go with us. One young girl kept stepping out of the procession and shouting, 'Workers of the world unite!!!' and we shouted, 'Hurrah!!' The policemen didn't stir, they were very serious."

Anna Pöhland, wife of a German soldier

Flensburg, Germany, before the war. Far from the battlefields, even children experience war in the cities of Germany. In port cities like Flensburg sailors line the streets. In cities near the front it is mostly soldiers. In Schneidemühl, the home town of Elfriede Kuhr, in the summer of 1915 it is often pilots. Based in Schneidemühl are the Albatross factories which produce aeroplanes for the war, as well as *Fliegerersatzabteilung*, in which pilots are trained.

"Yesterday a lieutenant in pilot's uniform greeted me. I turned bright red. Then he introduced himself. 'My name is Werner Waldecker and I'm from Bielefeld.' I was speechless and couldn't think of a thing to say, but just looked at him. I must have looked as stupid as possible. I never know what I'm supposed to say in such moments, and afterwards I'm furious with myself. When we parted, he kissed my hand and asked if he might hope to see me again. He has blue eyes and soft blond hair."

Elfriede Kuhr, German schoolgirl

Ostend, Belgium, c. 1915. For people who live near the front, the billeting of front-line soldiers soon becomes normality. Billeted soldiers are tolerated, of necessity, in the occupied territories of France, Germany and Russia.

"*The next day, Friday, the Great Man was quartered on us, the staff officers finding some place else to sleep, coming only to meals. I had hoped to be let alone, that it would not be necessary to serve; but I was not allowed that luxury. It was necessary to serve coffee, and look pleased with doing so. After the meal, I showed the workings of the samovar to the detestable Max and left. The Great Man paid little attention to me, except to greet me courteously. I could have done with less courtesy if he had given different orders to the army. All the misery, the awful orders, came from him, the* schrecklichkeit *we were face to face with. By his orders, the prisoners were cruelly deprived of food, and the levies were laid upon the people. When a man's personality weighs down those about him with a hopeless depression, in Poland they say, 'he sits on my head'. It is a wonderfully expressive phrase. The Great Man 'sat on my head' very heavily.*"

Laura de Gozdawa Turczynowicz, an American woman living in occupied Russian Poland

Postcard, France, c. 1915. Billeted French soldiers have it easier. The western front, where most of them are stationed, runs almost entirely through France. So they are mostly billeted on their compatriots.

Werner Waldecker, 1915. Flight Lieutenant Werner Waldecker – in training in Schneidemühl in Eastern Germany – tries to win the favours of Elfriede Kuhr. She isn't alone. Every girl at her school, she writes, has a pilot or soldier as a boyfriend.

"During three days we are kept near the enemy, living in well-constructed shelters which we improve each time we come back to them; then we have three days a little back of the front, and finally three days lodged in a nearby village, generally the same one. So we are leading a sort of humdrum existence, at least, for the moment, and are getting somewhat acquainted with the civil population, which has had a pretty hard time of it. These people are good souls, especially the dear old dame in whose house I am writing you. She was my hostess the other time we stopped in this village, and she is doing everything in her power to try and make me feel at home. But, dear Mama, what brings home back to me is what I have in my heart."

Anonymous French soldier

"We went home in the red 'railcar', as they call the little railway between Königsblick and Schneidemühl, and arrived in Schneidemühl with a lot of other excursionists at seven in the evening. When we parted by our front steps, Werner Waldecker said into my ear, 'I love you!' I looked at him, but I only said 'Thank you!' Then I jumped in the air with joy. Only I could be as silly as that!"

Elfriede Kuhr, German schoolgirl

Hikers at Dorfer-Thal, in the eastern Alps, before the war. As the food supply in the cities of Germany and Austria-Hungary worsens with the passing years of war, many city-dwellers travel to outlying villages in the hope of buying food there illegally, without ration cards.

"At noon I found the farmer's wife at home. She was very kind and friendly, though she herself has plenty of troubles. Her husband has for weeks been lying wounded in a hospital at the front. Her eldest child is ten years old, there are three younger ones, and another is on the way. She cannot cope with the work, the fields are untilled. There are no farm labourers, and the girls are all running off to the munition factories. 'If only my husband were at home.' She sympathized with my troubles and pitied me, for, after all, she has more to eat than I have. She packed bread, flour, beans, bacon and honey into my hand-basket, as much as I could carry. The prices which she charged me were moderate. She advised me not to go through the town, but to take the path across the fields to the station in order to avoid the police. 'They are very down on the hamsterers [hoarders].'"

Anna Eisenmenger, middle-class Austrian woman in Vienna

Postcard, Germany, c. 1914. For the women at home, the worst thing about the war is the uncertainty – are their husbands, brothers, sons still alive? Are they wounded, captured, or even dead? Often all they know about the horrors at the front are the countless wounded.

"It's as if the horror lived around us, and we would like to go in search of the Lord God. Day and night cars dash through our town and stretchers wobble through the streets. All full of wounded men. They are coming from the east, they're on the road for six days, and broken, body and soul. Transports are supposed to be coming from the western front tomorrow, and also lots of Frenchmen. And on the whole front in the west the most terrible battles are raging. Where is Kurt, and how is he doing?"

Elisabeth Kreiter, German soldier's mother

Mönkebergstrasse, Hamburg, before the war. As well as the uncertainty of how their dearest ones are doing at the front, for the relatives who stay behind there is also uncertainty of when they will see them again. No end to the war is in sight – the only hope is very occasional furlough.

Rostock, before the war. With the men serving at the front, women have to replace the workforce at home. But in most European countries, women are second-class citizens: they can't vote or own bank accounts without their husbands' permission. In England, many upper-class women become volunteer workers – which would have been unthinkable before the war.

"February 16. Leave. The day has been fixed twice before. Twice: block on all leave! And then? Then ten days in a row, two hundred and forty hours. The day before yesterday Germany, at the table with the white tablecloth, between mother and father, embarrassed to say a word – yesterday in the train, among silent soldiers. Now here. There had been leave? There was nothing more than a film, shot too quickly, clumsily edited, overwrought, overheated, torn into little pictures, into scraps. Lines of slogans, disconnected, unfathomable. Confusion without order or law."

Edlef Köppen, German soldier

"Then we heard that Women Police were badly needed, so we went off to their offices to see what that was like. All the WPs we saw looked very smart in a very dapper uniform of navy blue. We were interviewed by an inspector who gave us the full details. The work consists of the following duties. Searching incoming workers for matches, cigarettes, spirits etc. Searching outgoing workers for stolen property. Keeping guard at the gate and allowing no one to enter without a pass. Conducting visitors and new workers into the factory, dealing with lost passes, lost clocking cards... Patrolling to see there is no larking or slacking. We take turns at all these various jobs..."

Gabrielle M. West, British policewoman

◄ Rostock, before the war.
For the German population, as here in Rostock, finding basic supplies of food and fuel becomes more and more difficult. For Ethel Cooper, living as an Australian 'behind enemy lines', it soon becomes simply impossible.

"Gas is being cut off… There are no candles to be had, no petroleum and no spirits, so how one is to cook, let alone have a lighted room, I don't know. But as I say, the condition of things is so hopeless that it is not worth while thinking about it – much less worrying about it. The renowned German efficiency seems to fail miserably when it comes to social rather than military matters."

Ethel Cooper, Australian piano teacher living in Germany

Postcard, Germany, c. 1916. This German propaganda postcard shows smiling officers at home on leave. But, after two years of war, they have all seen too much death to truly smile. There is hardly a family in one of the countries involved that has not lost a beloved husband, son, brother or friend. The first loss is a terrible experience for those left at home.

"When I entered the classroom, Greta Dalüge and Trude Jakobi stepped apart. They had shocked faces and they were very embarrassed. I asked, 'What's going on?' Trude Jakobi stammered: 'Don't you know? Werner Waldecker has crashed.' 'Dead?' 'Yes. Dead.' I pushed my book bag under my desk and slowly took my coat off as if nothing had happened. After a while I could speak again and asked if they knew anything more. 'About the accident,' I said. But all they knew was that Waldecker had taken off from the airfield and crashed shortly afterwards. 'Alone?' 'Yes. Those things are useless, you said so yourself. So did Waldecker. Those planes.'"

Elfriede Kuhr, German schoolgirl

Postcard, France. 'Marrainage' is the name of a system created in France by the church and the boulevard press. Front soldiers were to be put in contact with young women from home to raise their morale. The women send little packages, letters, photographs. The honourable 'marrainage' soon turns into an obvious network for flirts and sexual contacts. There are similar schemes in all other fighting countries.

Postcard, France, c. 1916. The newspapers are soon full of thousands of contact advertisements – both from soldiers and from women at home. It is no longer the case by any means that both parties are unmarried. When such 'immoral activity' takes the upper hand, the authorities step in.

"Letter from a soldier's wife, publication forbidden:
'As most women display the results that the men on furlough have left behind, and are already looking forward to the next war boy, I too have no wish to be left out and laughed at. I too wish to support patriotism. But I also don't want to take the wrong path, I do want to practise German fidelity, because my husband too has been in the field since the start of the war. But nature demands her own rights. I also hope that my plan will be fulfilled, and what our result will bring only the future will tell. For our Kaiser also needs soldiers. These furlough visits cannot go on for too long, because otherwise the war will be over and our plans for a war boy will be thwarted – Yours faithfully…'"

Edlef Köppen, Army Report

"It is beneath the dignity of an officer to appear in uniform with dubious female company in the street or in inns or restaurants; he lacks tact when, so accompanied, he seeks out, in uniform, hostelries where he can expect to meet comrades with their ladies – cabarets, bars, night cafés and similar venues – is a slur on our dress of honour. The Commander."

V. Bonin, Lieutenant General

A village in France, before the war. Before the war, the role of women in Europe had been clearly defined. They had to take care of their families – as on this French beach. As second-class citizens, many professions were closed to them and women didn't have the vote in most countries in Europe. As a result of the war, which tears many men away from home, women suddenly find themselves in jobs that were previously meant only for men, including service in the police. But genuine equality is still a long way off.

"Training lasts a fortnight and consists of lectures, attendance at police courts and children's courts and taking notes of the cases heard. Drill, patrolling in the evenings and a few other jobs. We patrol with a WP sergeant round Victoria, and other lively neighbourhoods. One day we went to Paddington district where two WP are permanently employed… We watched them at work. They help the school children across the roads. See children are not taken into pub houses, report broken area railings, people sleeping in basements, etc… But we haven't been near a factory, or heard anything about factory work, which seems odd."

Gabrielle M. West, British female police officer in training

Berlin, Germany, 4 September 1915. One popular way of collecting money from the civilian population in Germany is called 'nailing'. Wooden figures are erected, into which – for a small sum of money – nails can be hammered. The most famous of these statues is the 'Iron Hindenburg' in Berlin.

"On the first day of school we start engaging the girl pupils in relief work. Two collecting tins are set up, one for the Red Cross, one for war aid. Each child brings his or her own donation. Quite at their discretion, of course, quite voluntarily, as all compulsion is forbidden. But neither is it necessary. Everyone is so happy to give! Fabrics are bought with the money that has been brought in already. Some children bring whole bales of wool and linen materials from their parents' shops. The youngest girls help by working in the soup kitchen and canning fruit for a few hours in the afternoon, in other hours they stitch shirts for the wounded, while girls from the middle years knit socks, scarves, abdominal bandages and wrist-warmers for the soldiers."

Jakob Loewenberg, German headmaster and author

Soldiers stationed at the rail yard, Lille, France, c. 1916.
As food supplies decline in Germany, youth criminality rises sharply in the course of the war and forces the German government to intervene.

"Yesterday came this new order – it is really interesting. Under eighteen years old, nobody is allowed to go alone to cafés, tea-rooms, automats, restaurants, or cinematographs, not allowed to smoke or receive alcoholic drinks, not allowed to be out after ten in the evening without a good reason. And when they go to cinematographs which are specially advertised as 'for young people', the sexes have to sit separated!"

Ethel Cooper, Australian piano teacher in Leipzig

Scottish postcard, c. 1915. Scottish nurse Sarah Macnaughtan leaves Belgium in June 1915 and goes back to London, where she reports on her experiences in a series of lectures – and campaigns for the war.

"We had meetings every night in Glasgow. They were mostly badly organized and well attended. Here I have an agent arranging everything, and two of my meetings have been enormous. The first was at the dock-gates in the open air, and the second in the Town Hall. The band of the Welch Regiment played, and Mr Glover conducted, but nothing is the same, of course. Alan is at Porthcawl, and came to see me this morning. The war news could hardly be worse, and yet I am told by men who get sealed information from the Foreign Office that worse is coming. Poor Russia! She wants help more than anyone. Her wounded are quite untended. I go there next month. The King of the Belgians has made me Chevalier de l'Ordre de Léopold."

Sarah Macnaughtan, Scottish volunteer nurse

German postcard, c. 1915. Providing food for millions of war widows and orphans puts an unprecedented strain on the welfare systems of countries involved in the war. Since 1907 there has been a law in Germany providing for the widows and orphans of fallen soldiers. But in practice the families lose not only their men, but also their perspective on life and the material basis of their existence.

"Three years ago Jacek was still alive. I cuddled up close to him, he loved me, he was alive. These days I am dead inside, I have no heart, no feelings, no faith, no hope. I feel no physical pain, I no longer need anything, I do not pity anyone, no one's unhappiness moves me, I have no compassion."

Helena Jabłońska, Polish widow under siege in Przemyśl

France, before the war. As the war progresses, many farmers in the belligerent countries are assigned prisoners of war to replace men at the front. But they have to be both guarded and paid.

France, before the war. In spite of food cards, prices on the markets in Germany and Austria-Hungary continue to rise. The governments establish maximum prices, but that measure only encourages the black market. Hunger prevails, above all in the cities, at least since the winter of 1917.

"Yesterday we were in Münchehagen. Such misery among the small farmers. When we were outside, the opera singer's wife said to me, 'Now you see, the Germans make such a fuss about our conditions in Russia, is this any different?' These farmers have twenty acres of land, four cows, one horse, chickens and pigs; the wife has to take care of it almost alone. Then she may get a prisoner to help her. For that she will have to pay 1 mark a day and his keep."

Anna Pöhland, wife of a German soldier

"Now Lotte has left as well, and our house is quiet again. When and under what circumstances will we see each other again? One doesn't dare to think beyond the day. The only certainty is that war, this terrible war, continues to rage, destroying and despoiling everything. When and how will it end? Often we lack the most basic necessities; maximum prices are established, only to be greatly exceeded. The farmers have goods to excess, the maximum prices mean nothing to them, and they only bring out their products if they are paid for them to excess. And the government can do nothing to stop them. A pair of shoes costs 30 marks. Why can not order be restored to this chaos?"

Elisabeth Kreiter, mother of a German soldier

Rural idyll, France, before the war. In both Britain and France tens of thousands of ammunition factories have been built from scratch, to satisfy the insatiable hunger of the armies. Here hundreds of thousands of women, many from the countryside, find employment that provides them with an income so they can feed their families. But working conditions in these quickly constructed factories are often extremely dangerous.

"*The particles of acid land on your face and make you nearly mad, like pins and needles only much more so; and they land on your clothes and make brown specks all over them, and they rot your handkerchiefs and get up your nose and down your throat, and into your eyes so that you are blind and speechless by the time your hour is up and you make your escape. All over the middle section are notices telling you what to do if anyone swallows brown fumes. 'If conscious give an emetic. If blue in the face, apply artificial respiration. If very blue, oxygen.' I'm sure I must have swallowed countless brown fumes.*"

Gabrielle M. West, female police officer in an ammunitions factory

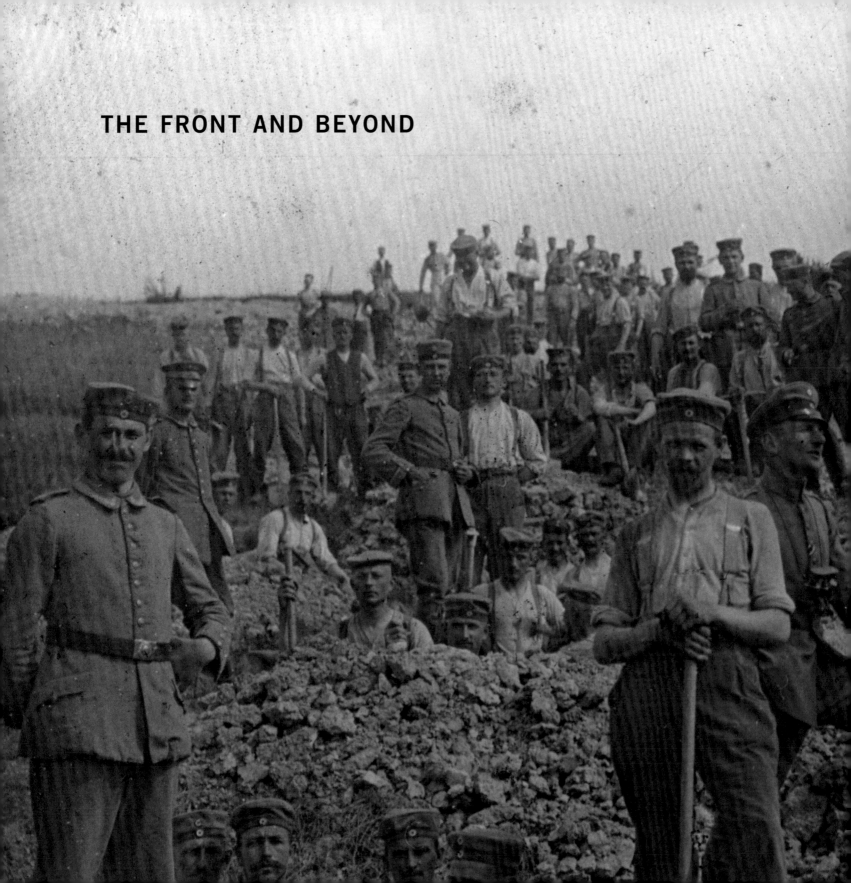

THE FRONT AND BEYOND

"At last I got my first postcard from home, which delighted my heart
and brought me consolation. Receiving a sign of life
after such a long time."

Karl Kasser, Austrian prisoner of war in Siberia

German officers sorting mail in a dugout in Warneton, Belgium. It
is the responsibility of officers like these to write to the families of
a fallen soldier to inform them of his death.

The trenches were part of everyday life in the Great War. In the American Civil War, from 1861–1865, trenches had been excavated in which enemy soldiers waited opposite each other. But no one expected that to happen in Europe. The French soldiers wanted to get to Berlin as quickly as possible, while the Germans were convinced they had already reached Paris when they attacked Belgium without encountering any great resistance. The English nurse Edith Cavell, who was tending to the international war injured in Brussels, reported in a letter to the *Nursing Mirror* that the German soldiers were amazed when they encountered Belgians in Belgium, as they were certain they were already in Paris.

The German trenches on the western front, in Flanders and on the Somme, were made deeper and more stable as time passed. Wood and cement was brought in from the occupied territories on the eastern front, enabling entire settlements to be established below ground, connected to one another through subterranean passageways. Down there, the soldiers were relatively secure even when the opposing side shot grenades. In the summer of 1916, British soldiers were surprised to discover that there were some survivors in the trenches even after days of shell fire. The German soldiers were deaf, blind and had lost their minds, but suffered no other injuries from the explosions.

In 1916, workers from English and Australian coal mines began to be employed for the construction of tunnels. Several trenches of the kind had already been excavated on the Somme. The tunnels constructed in the difficult ground of Flanders were a masterpiece of mining. In 1917, tunnels of up to thirty metres below ground and eight kilometres long were dug near Messines in western Flanders, ending beneath German lines. Nineteen explosive devices were detonated at the end of the mines, and the craters can still be seen today. The largest bomb had a weight of 42 tonnes, and the explosion could be heard in London and, allegedly, even in Ireland.

German soldiers in their trenches in occupied France. On the western front, trenches often run – as they do here – between or even through ruined houses.

If new tactics for approaching enemy lines were not employed, the attackers were awaited on the other side by machine-gun fire. When they were successful in advancing, as in the German attacks of 1914 and 1917, or the Russian offensive of 1916 under General Alexej Brusilov, the connection to supply units was quickly interrupted. Unless there were Allied camps nearby that could be plundered, the soldiers soon suffered from hunger and thirst. Plundering was part of everyday life in the war. After the capture of Romania in 1917, more than two million tonnes of grains, 100,000 cattle and 200,000 goats and pigs were seized and sent to Germany to ensure that there was no repeat of the famine winter of 1916–17. Instead, it was the Romanian people who now suffered from starvation. Compared to conditions for countries of the Central Powers, there were hardly any shortages in Britain at all. In October 1917, a German agent from London reported that an amble through the department stores of

Austro-Hungarian soldiers having lunch on the eastern front. The longer the war lasts, the more disastrous the supply situation of the Austro-Hungarian army.

(*Opposite*) Austrian cavalry – uhlans and dragoons – on their way to the Russian front. The First World War is the last war in which cavalry advances against the enemy with spear and sabre.

Harrods, Whiteleys and Fortnum & Mason, or the markets at Billingsgate, Smithfield and Covent Garden, would have been incredibly depressing for a German. The shelves and stalls were full with produce, he said, and showed that there was no shortage of goods in Britain at all. The unrestrained submarine battle with which the German navy hoped to starve the British may have done some damage, but it didn't affect the food supply.

Admittedly, living conditions on the home front were also dependent on social circumstances. In Russia and Germany there were demonstrations and food crises even by the second year of the war. In Paris, the seamstresses of the Paris haute couture went on strike in the spring of 1917. The workers were soon joined other industries, including the armament industry. By May, more than 20,000 women were on strike, while the male workers were unable to strike because they were obligated to serve in the factories for military purposes. Soldiers began to join forces with the women by demonstrating in their own way. From 29 April there were mutinies amongst those units which, after a disastrous defeat at Chemin des Dames, were due to be sent back into battle. The demands of the soldiers were simple: they wanted more home leave and a halt to those offensives that they saw as pointless from the outset, as at Chemin des Dames. There were also pacifist and socialist-revolutionary motives that found expression in the French anti-military song *Chanson de Craonne*: In the '*guerre infâme*' soldiers saw themselves as 'the damned', as the 'victims' ordered to 'defend the property of the ruling powers' who were 'financing the war with others' lives'.

A report by the *Service de renseignements des armées* from 30 May 1917 described the morale of the troops as good, but the soldiers' letters to their families displayed a more menacing side. They wrote that hundreds of

thousands of comrades had fallen, and that the younger officers were arrogant and brutal. The 'capitalists' were sending their own people out to be slaughtered in order to line their own pockets, said others, and that Germany had offered peace numerous times in vain. In the end the only option would be revolution, as the Russians had already done. All of this was reason enough to warrant the dismissal of the existing commander-in-chief of the French troops, General Robert Nivelle. Philippe Pétain was put in his place, a man who was able to discipline the soldiers again with a blend of punishments and promises. One year later, the same symptoms appeared amongst

German soldiers. Their commander-in-chief was not dismissed, however, but lost his nerve and gave up the battle which was, in any case, already lost.

Nonetheless, some effort was made to lift the soldiers' moods. Under the regulations that the commander-in-chief and field railway chief were held to, the soldiers were to receive newspapers and patriotic literature from their home countries. Painters, photographers and cinematographers were also active on the front in order to document the everyday lives of the soldiers and convey the feeling that their heroism wouldn't go unnoticed. 'In this way, the leaders and heroes of the army are brought consistently and successfully closer through the public spirit,' declared secret service chief Walter Nikolai.

Even more successful than the German war press office was the British film industry, which on 21 August 1916 brought *The Battle of the Somme* into the country's five thousand cinemas, exactly seven weeks after the start of the battle. By the end

Hundreds of German soldiers digging a 'defence trench' on the western front in France. Trenches were originally an invention of private soldiers to protect themselves against the murderous artillery of the enemy.

(*Opposite*) Soldiers making lunch on the western front in Belgium. Many diaries from the First World War complain about the miserable quality of food in the trenches.

of its opening week, a million Londoners had seen the film. Six months later, so had half the British population. Copies were exported to eighteen countries. It was a realistic portrayal of the attack, depicting the falling soldiers. In one London cinema, the orchestra even stopped playing during this scene. It was the first time that the general public had been subjected to something approaching the true horrors of war.

The daily life of soldiers is the central concern for August Fuhrmann during the First World War. His photographs show soldiers playing cards, reading the post – and eternally waiting. Again, Fuhrmann shows only comparatively beautiful images of the war to the audience at home. But a closer reading of the faces of the soldiers shows the remains of the terror in their eyes, unhidden from view.

June/July 1916. A page from the diary of F. Southon, a sapper with the 12th Field Company Royal Engineers, on the western front. The hole in the diary is most likely a bullet hole. He does not explain how it came to be here, but as he writes around it, he may not have been injured.

June

25 Pontoon bridging at the village of Herneim.
26 Putting the village of Recques in a tempory [sic] state of defence.
27 Pontoon drill and raft making.
28 Pontoon bridging at Polincove village.
29 Rowing exercise and route marching.
30 Bridging competition between sections. No. 4 winning by 8 points, No. 2 second. 25 frcs prize, with another 25 frcs added by section officer for winning.

July

1 Rapid barbed wiring practices.
2 Paraded at 3am and left Polincove marched to Audruicq to entrain for Doullens arrived after 8hrs journey then marched back to the village of Ribeaucourt arrived there at 11 o' clock at night.
3 Left Ribeaucourt at 8 o'clock and tracked on with the Brigade for 6 hrs stopping at the village of Havernas for the rest of the day.
4 Rested during the day and left Havernas at 7:39 pm and marched on to Bertangles arriving...

▶ **Carpathian Mountains, c. 1916.** Soldiers peeling potatoes. Providing for millions of soldiers at the front is a huge logistical challenge. New methods of preserving and packaging foods on a mass scale are developed – the start of the modern 'ration'.

"Our lunch gets more wretched from day to day. Yesterday for example there was thick pearl barley cooked in rather smelly pork. I couldn't find any meat, but there was a whole pear in it. Today there was rice with pears again. Additionally, there was some tinned liver sausage this evening, although it must have contained a damned small amount of liver. Most of it was probably groats, potato flour and the like. It tasted terrible. I spread my bread with artificial honey instead. We're getting barely half as much butter as before. If there's cheese, four men now get as much as one did before. On the other hand, last night there were rotten herrings. You can have no idea how much that is doing for war morale."

Robert Pöhland, German soldier, in a letter to his wife

Russian Poland, c. 1916. Every war needs heroes – and many of those who go to war in the summer of 1914 want to be heroes. The truth looks different. On the German side, the ultimate mark of heroism is the 'Blue Max', the award 'Pour le Mérite'. In the First World War it is awarded 687 times – to generals, flying aces and ship commanders. Only two infantrymen are decorated, both lieutenants. There are no heroes among the private soldiers.

"*Boelcke and Immelmann got their Pour le Mérite for their eighth kill. I have twice that many. What's going to happen now? I was very excited. There were rumours that I was going to get a fighter squadron. Then one day the telegram arrives: 'Lieutenant v. R. made leader of fighter squadron 11.' I must say, I was annoyed. And I'd rather have had the Pour le Mérite. After two days – we're sitting comfortably with the Boelcke squadron celebrating my departure – when a telegram comes in from headquarters to say that his majesty has been so kind as to award me the Pour le Mérite. Of course I was overjoyed. It was a plaster on what had gone before.*"

Manfred von Richthofen, German pilot

Carpathian Mountains, c. 1916. Officer dugouts at the western front. The longer the war drags on, the more the soldiers come to dislike their officers. While the soldiers in the trenches often spend more time fighting rats, lice and illnesses than they do the enemy, the people who are sending them to their deaths are sleeping in the hinterland of the front, in comfortable beds – or even travelling to Paris, London or Berlin after the day's work or for the weekend.

"The revolver cannon are being withdrawn, I'm sent to a gun unit east of Verdun. The dense, green crowns of old beech trees cover us against enemy planes, we shoot, we're shot at, over all we live a peaceful, boring life. People only complain about the bad food, in the stables the paymaster and the sergeant eat fried steaks and fill their bellies, it makes for bad blood. Also the fact that the officers at rest are having a new mess built for themselves, while our dugouts are awash with rain, we lack boards and tarpaper. Or that near to our guns a concrete dugout is being built for the staff, with every comfort. 'Costs twenty thousand marks,' says a bricklayer, 'with that much money you could winter more than a war.'"

Ernst Toller, German poet and soldier

Belgium, c. 1916. The religions also put themselves completely at the service of the war. Army chaplains bless dying soldiers; bishops preach hatred of the enemy. And the soldiers are fine with anything that promises a little hope – there are few atheists in the trenches.

"My offering myself as war chaplain to the Provincial has had a wonderful effect on me. I long to go and shed my blood for Jesus and, if He wills it, to die a martyr of charity. The thought that at any moment I may be called to the Front, perhaps to die, has roused a great desire to do all I can while I have life. I feel great strength to make any sacrifice and little difficulty in doing so. I may not have long now to prove my love for Jesus."

Father William Doyle, chaplain with the 16th (Irish) Division

Warneton, Belgium, c. 1916. The soldiers at the front live in a different world. Bombed-out buildings are just as much a part of their everyday life as the trenches. Often the troops are billeted in such houses which, even though they have been blown apart, provide more comfort than many dugouts.

"At last I got my first postcard from home, which delighted my heart and brought me consolation. Receiving a sign of life after such a long time. Replied straight away and wrote asking for money and underwear and smoking material. We lacked a lot of things, if you could smoke it was better. It made it easier to bear hunger and cold."

Karl Kasser, Austrian prisoner of war in Siberia

"Still, we may win. The multitude of men who think of nothing but serving hard and faithfully unto death, who do not hope for distinctions or promotions, may carry the world into safety and a new life. Hundreds and thousands of them will die, after this Good Friday, more painfully than on a Cross. Our hope is that in them, as in Christ, a worse world may die into a better, and larger life come out of death, and mankind be ennobled by losing its noblest men – the old mystery of the Cross and of evolution."

C.E. Montague, British war correspondent

"Beside me I see a dark hole, stairs leading down to a bunker at the bottom. Black, damp and at any rate lousy, room for only three men. The orderlies lying in there won't let me in. I sit down again, crack open a tin of meat that was lying in front of me in the mud, and start chewing. It goes on raining for another half day; then I'm called out of the tunnel. As the entrance is already completely blocked with mud, I creep in on my belly. I slept like an animal."

Gerrit Engelke, German soldier, during the Battle of the Somme

Russia, c. 1916. The differences between officers and men in the First World War are enormous. While the privates sleep on planks, tormented by all kinds of vermin, officers often have comfortable dugouts of their own, or are billeted in confiscated houses.

Louppy, France, c. 1916. Much of the everyday life of soldiers in the First World War consists of waiting. They usually spend their free time behind the front, like these soldiers visiting the château at Louppy.

"Everything is new and blissful, warmth and silence and books and the words of friends, the attention of the landlady, the hot bath, the bed. Outside, I hadn't been out of my clothes, at night I slept on dank straw or on the cold, damp earth. After a year I had gone home for a short leave, and on the way, in Berlin, I stayed for twenty-four hours, I had rented a room in one of the comfortable palace hotels, I just wanted to rest for an hour, and then see the motley hubbub of the streets, cafés, shop windows, women, but when the white, cooling sheet buried me I forgot Berlin and stayed in bed for the whole twenty-four hours."

Ernst Toller, German soldier

"My dear Marie and my lovely niece Andrée. What a beautiful day!!! And how happy we are, duties accomplished, to be in peace and tranquillity!!!! I will imagine I'm in Nice, that we're both lying in the sun and almost everyone is writing to their families to reassure and encourage them, others sleep, while others have gone off to get the deliveries done.

The colonel issued me with an extract from the army corps order for 14 March 1915. You'll find the same announcement in the Army Bulletin. I'm very happy. You'll find the extract in question enclosed. As soon as you've read it, send it to my wife, who will keep it for my son. I forgot to tell you that this quotation will be inscribed in my passbook and that it will give me a right to the Croix de Guerre (a decoration that can't be bought with money). All my officers are happy with me and I'm filled with courage."

Maurice Aupetit, French soldier

France, 1918. Senior officers of all participating nations generally experience the war from their command posts, dozens – or even hundreds – of kilometres away from actual battle. Still, both they and, even more, the politicians of all the countries involved want to experience 'real war' at close range at the front. Since that is, of course, too dangerous, such visits are staged down to the smallest details.

"I feel a kind of grudge against the mere sightseer who comes out to see the war as a sort of show, accompanied by all sorts of luxury and petting. It seems they were rather scared at the place I had brought them to on Sunday, where the shells were falling about, and I have been rebuked, not very gravely, for imperilling the army's guests – not very gravely, because I think we all feel in our hearts that the sightseer's only chance of saving his soul alive is that he should get a taste, if only for a few minutes, of the kind of thing that our soldiers are bearing all day."

C.E. Montague, British war correspondent

▶ **Dining salon on the Emperor's yacht *Hohenzollern*, before the war.** After the battle of Skagerrak, the German navy spends most of the war in harbour. The class difference between officers and sailors is considerably more marked than it is among the army in the field.

"A Russian naval mine was drifting there, half protruding from the water. We got about 500 metres away from it and immediately violently opened fire on it from our looted Russian guns. It nearly went badly wrong, because suddenly there was a dull rumble and a column of water rose up in front of us. I was able to explain the situation to the commander to my own satisfaction. A few seconds after the explosion the surface of the water was covered with dead fish over a wide radius. I never forgave our commander for the fact that out of a very short-sighted and self-important sense of duty he wouldn't let us collect this delicious and welcome addition to our supplies, but had us set course and leave immediately."

Joachim Ringelnatz, German sailor and author

Russian Poland, c. 1916. While at the beginning of the war there were daily skirmishes even on the western front, after that the threat of an attack – by the enemy, or ordered by one's own supreme command – remains constant, but in between there isn't much for the soldiers to do.

"*I have had your dear letter of the 9th, in which you speak of our home. It makes me happy to feel how fine and strong is the force of life which soon adjusts itself to each separation and uprooting. It makes me happy, too, to think that my letters find an echo in your heart. Sometimes I was afraid of boring you, because though our life is so fine in many ways, it is certainly very primitive, and there are not many salient things to relate.*"

Anonymous French soldier

France, c. 1916. The human spirit is incredibly good at getting used to even the strangest circumstances. As bizarre, for example, as artillery duels fought over the heads of the soldiers in the trenches.

Lille, France, c. 1915. Cities under occupation have to come to terms with the new conditions. This also includes the constant presence of the military police, who are supposed to ensure calm and order in the occupied territories.

"*Not a man was in sight, nor a house, nor gun, not even a trench, yet we were, as a matter of fact, in the middle of a battlefield. From where we stood it was not more than a mile to the English trenches and only two miles to Neuve Chapelle; and even as we stood there, from behind us, from a battery we had passed without seeing, came a crash and then the long spinning roar of something milling down aisles of air, and a far-off detonation from the direction of Neuve Chapelle. Tssee-ee-rr… Bong! over our heads from the British lines came an answering wail, and in the field, a quarter of a mile beyond us, there was a geyser of earth, and slowly floating away a greenish-yellow cloud of smoke. From all over the horizon came the wail and crash of shells – an 'artillery duel', as the official reports call it, the sort of thing that goes on day after day.*"

Arthur Ruhl, American journalist with the German army

"*On the way back into the centre of town – we have to go up the steep hill in the midday heat – with our practised policeman eyes we see some suspicious individuals. We stop them, they can present IDs, we let them go, very much to the chagrin of the older comrades, who like arresting people. There's a lot of vivid activity in the market square: the sentries approach, companies move in, high generals stride across the square. Every time we get there our eyes take in the beautiful town hall with its fine gothic architecture. The old, magnificent cathedral rises up in the background. The streets that meet here fall away in all directions, we see green sections of landscape along the street.*"

Fritz Niebergall, German soldier

France, 1918. The soldiers currently on reserve spend their so-called free time behind the front. These breaks for recovery between periods in the trenches introduce a breath of normality into the soldier's life.

"Yesterday I used my free afternoon hours for a refreshing bath. Because such a thing is nowhere to be found nearby I went to France, in Wervicq there's actually a very nice bathing establishment in a big factory. You can soap yourself off under a shower first, then cool off nicely in big swimming basins. That was a great source of enjoyment for me. So I didn't mind the long journey (it's about two hours from here), particularly in the glorious weather we've had here since yesterday. On the way back I picked a lot of blackberries and didn't get home until it was quite dark."

Robert Pöhland, German soldier, in a letter to his wife

Béthencourt, France, c. 1916. Apart from field post from home, the soldiers in the trenches are kept regularly supplied with newspapers. These newspapers are produced specially for the soldiers and printed just behind the front. That means they can be even more strictly censored than newspapers at home.

"30 September 1916
My dear Désirée,
We've received reinforcements of 17 men for our company, 150 men for the regiment when we're 800 short, some reinforcement!
  The weather's nice, it feels good to be resting. It said in the paper that front soldiers have a right to seven days' leave rather than six.
  It's always nice to have an extra 24 hours at home, but my leave is still a long way off.
In the place where we are there are still some civilians who are very nice to us. I don't know where my brother Charles is because he's like me, he changes his base camp a lot.
  He'll have to go on leave soon.
Your friend, who thinks about you often, who gives you kisses for ever."

Auguste 'Maurice' Lecourt, French soldier

Montmedy, France, c. 1916.
In the First World War the task of delivering field post to prisoners of war is undertaken by the Red Cross. Volunteer helpers also distribute parcels with charitable donations, as shown here, to soldiers at the front. For soldiers without families this is their only chance of receiving parcels from home.

"My dear, kind wife! The blackcurrants were quite rotten, and I had to throw them all away. A thick, sticky goo. The juice had seeped through the round box into the sugar and dissolved it. A nice disappointment for me, you can imagine. To send berries you would need a little basket that the air can get to, otherwise they are always bound to spoil. None the less, thank you for your good intentions, and for your letter and the magazine."

Robert Pöhland, German soldier, in a letter to his wife

Russian Poland, c. 1916. Many of those in the trenches, particularly the young volunteers, have no wives at home. None the less they yearn for warmth and security. Brothels are set up on all fronts in the war, for both privates and officers, and many soldiers have affairs with women living in the hinterland of the front.

"That ensign, Herr Sporer, is a wonderful pianist. While the others were out drinking, I stayed in the music room. I was overwhelmed by sadness. I can't get Maria out of my mind. For a moment I thought about giving myself up, so that I could search for her all over Italy, just to spend one more night with her."

Anonymous Austrian officer, whose diary was found on the battlefield

France, c. 1916. Horses play a very important role in the First World War, both in providing supplies for the troops and as a means of transport. In the course of the war, however, they are increasingly replaced by bicycles.

"The procession begins, and afterwards the colonel delivers a general compliment to everybody and gives us permission to meet up individually.

So I cut short my conversation with the other telephone operator decorated the same day as me because it's after midday and we have to meet up, there's a banquet waiting for us but there is one problem which is that our adjutant and our telephone operator each have a bicycle and there's about 14 km to do. Also, knowing I'm a good horseman, the adjutant phones through to ask the lieutenant for permission to have his horse saddled up for me. Permission is granted and there's Maurice on horseback."

Maurice Aupetit, French soldier

Western front, during the war. American soldiers in a grenade attack. The standard rifle is an infantryman's main weapon. In trench warfare, however, it is often too big and clumsy. Here the hand grenade rules. It isn't the explosion as such that make them so dangerous, but the shrapnel, all the little splinters fired in all directions. In the cramped conditions in the trenches, or in a dugout, the hand grenade is a deadly weapon.

"We're still firing off to the right, sight 750. And behold, there's old Peter Carsten, minstrel, Holsteiner: hand grenades in his fists, jumps up top and shouts 'Let's get going!' He tumbles back into the trench with a shot to the pelvis, white as a sheet."

Gerrit Engelke, German soldier, during the Battle of the Somme

Russian Poland, c. 1916. The German Army Report is published daily out of General Headquarters. It contains accounts of all the most important events on all the fronts. The reports are always censored and enhanced, but they still convey a direct picture of the war.

"Rainy weather today. Silent artillery – and I too (dispatch runner) have a degree of peace. It was just as desirable as necessary after the fighting of 20–25 June. (Which you may have read about under the name Vauxaillon in the Army Report.) In our damp hole in the ground (meaning: sleeping on down feathers) I even dreamed! O sentimentality! One about dear, dear, sunny Faaborg in Denmark, two, about feinbrot with lashings of whipped cream (casual click of the tongue!), three, about huge great waves, in which I was shivering near Ostende. You see: the imagination works like a gramophone."

Gerrit Engelke, German worker poet and soldier

Using a trench 'periscope', Russian Poland, c. 1916. The war throws together men of very different origins who are now forced to spend a long time together, often in very cramped conditions. This can produce curious friendships – but sometimes the men are too different to get on with each other.

Russian Poland, c. 1916. To get themselves through the long wait, whether as here, in the trenches, or on standby in the hinterland, German soldiers like to play cards, particularly the game *skat*. Card-playing is so important that playing cards are declared strategic goods, and are still produced even in times of great need.

"If only I could sometimes hear a single word of praise, but there isn't such a thing here. My own comrades are always making fun of me because I'm different from them. This morning, when we went to work at dead of night, I deliberately walked a few paces behind the unit so as not to have the glorious morning air poisoned by tobacco smoke, and not to have to listen to the stupid, childish, idiotic chatter. I almost always do this, by the way. I've sometimes got a tongue-lashing from my superiors, because we all have to be led around like sheep. One NCO has to walk at the front, one at the back, just as sheepdogs keep the herd together. These group leaders also have the same instinct as sheepdogs. I heard the following conversation of a pioneer with this NCO: 'So why does he' (meaning me) 'always go at the back?' The NCO replied, 'He seems to be depressed.' But the pioneer said, 'Oh him, he's mad.'"

Robert Pöhland, German soldier, in a letter to his wife

"With shining helmets, the black, white and red band on our arms – the mark of our power – we leave the guardroom. Today we have our last, third number. It is a hot, glorious afternoon in May. Everything sparkles and gleams in the sun. Slowly we approach our guardroom again, where the next number is already coming towards us. In spite of the heat the stove is burning, our comrades are drinking hot coffee. We always read, play cards, shout and have good conversations."

Fritz Niebergall, German soldier

France, c. 1916. A soldier with a medal of the Légion d'honneur. The Légion d'honneur, founded by Napoleon I in 1802, is France's highest decoration. In the First World War it is awarded over 55,000 times.

"A good man, was our compatriot, for he had a very recent Legion of Honour pinned upon his breast. He had been put with a few men on Hill 285, a sort of volcano stuffed with mines, and was told to telephone when he needed relief. He refused to telephone and remained there for three weeks."

Arthur Conan Doyle, British author

France, 1918. In the course of the war, orders of merit become a means of propaganda. Thus the order of the Légion d'honneur is awarded to a messenger pigeon that brought a desperate request from a group of encircled soldiers to headquarters, but died the same day.

"This morning, I took advantage of our rest to go to the hospital for the severely injured eight kilometres from here to see one of my men, the poor chap has been operated on four times in eight days and will have to go through it again because he's got osteitis.

He was happy to see me and even though he was in a fever he gave me a warm welcome. I recommended him to his nurse, he's a good soldier, he's even very brave. An hour before he was wounded I had told him off, he'd got up on top of a shelter a few metres from the boche trenches. I gave him a few francs and a Sacred Heart medal.

It's all the more worthy of interest that when Lille was occupied by the Germans he was in convalescence, having had his leg broken and to get away from them he escaped from Lille through the sewers."

Alexandre Jacqueau, French soldier

"It is isn't impossible, my dear parents, that the storm is approaching for us. You know what that means. I would only like to say a few words about it. More and more I see what I had in my parents. I would like to express my warmest thanks to you for all the love with which you have surrounded me, dear parents! Here, where it is so stupidly obvious that a piece of iron could strike me at any minute, we learn to believe in God and a personal life in the beyond. Otherwise one couldn't bear it. But let's hope that we will be reunited safe and sound."

Fritz Niebergall, German soldier, in a letter to his parents

Monfalcone, Italy, 1917. After successful battles, like the battle of Caporetto, booty is brought together at collection points.

Belgium, c. 1916. Where possible the central powers deploy enemy weapons again at the front – like this British hand grenade, being examined by German soldiers.

"A glorious victory was reported at Metz. Three army corps beaten, over fifty guns captured. As gratifying as that was, it also made me envious. By now I had made a formal request for a ship to the Baltic, mentioning that I knew about the area. Heaven knows what waste-paper basket that request ended up in."

Joachim Ringelnatz, German sailor and author

"Here we haven't a moment, a moment of peace; they're even rare when we're resting. As to B... des C..., life there is unbearable, being subjected to incessant bombing. Often the communiqués make us laugh when they talk about fighting with bombs and grenades. In that case we should be in the communiqué every day because as well as the artillery bombardments, this battle of bombs, grenades, shells, trenches, torpedoes and mine launchers is at B... des C... all the time."

Alexandre Jacqueau, French soldier

Russian Poland, c. 1915. Soldiers resting in the forest. No soldier can endure life in the trenches for long, so front units rotate between the trenches and the hinterland, where there are distractions for the soldiers – alcohol and brothels. But it isn't a normal life, and can't satisfy the longing for home.

"Because you so kindly offered, along with Marie, to bring my mail to Paul and Louise, I will take advantage of the fact to add a long letter for them. Unless your letter has got lost. As I wrote in my last letter my trousers suit me marvellously well, and with the puttees, a cap and a new greatcoat I look like a raw recruit (apart from my white hair). The fact is that I was a bit ragged. Damn it, the sun called for clean clothes and the sector where we've been for almost a month and a half is very calm also we take advantage of the fact to wash ourselves it's hardly luxurious if the heat lasts a week I'm hoping to sneak off to La Suippe which is about 500 metres from my post. There's complete (or indeed partial) balneotherapy there, and central heating in winter. Well that didn't stop me escaping without even a hint of a cold."

Maurice Aupetit, French soldier

Galicia, Austria-Hungary, c. 1915. Good communication between commanders and privates has been one of the most important keys to victory since ancient times. Communications are revolutionized in the First World War. The telephone is deployed as a weapon for the first time – to report attacks, or issue orders. But since the telephone wires are often severed by enemy artillery, as well as by gnawing rats, 'telephonists' – like those pictured – constantly have to lay new wires between the command posts.

"Today, Corpus Christi, feast of the Friend par excellence. We were relieved of our posts at four o'clock this morning and I was able to go to mass when I got here and commune with you in my mind.

I won't write at greater length, because I spent part of the night by my telephone organizing artillery fire. I slept for barely two hours and those four days have made me quite tired and then I want to drop a line to Paulette. The weather is splendid and I am in admirably good health."

Alexandre Jacqueau, French soldier

▶ **Montfaucon, France, c. 1916.** Until the First World War, more soldiers are lost to illness than to battles. In order to curb illnesses in the field – and above all in the trenches – three new strategies are applied. In the Prussian army, they start to cut off the soldiers' hair. Along with regular delousing – another innovation – this helps to combat the lice that pass on diseases. But the third and most important campaign is the maintenance of latrines, which have to be far from sources of drinking water and soldiers' accommodation.

"It's a great life here and I am as fit as a prizefighter. Last week we were digging trenches all day and every day, and it is fine, satisfying work, and the completed trench, with all its little cunning contraptions, a joy to its creators. We get up at 5.30, go by train to the scene of our labours, with a piece of bread in each man's haversack and six tins of bully beef to each company, eat our dinner on the grass and come home at 5.30 in the evening to wash ourselves and clean our kit and gear for next day, and get to sleep."

Sergeant C.E. Montague, in a letter to his friend Francis Vodd

Italy, 1917. The First World War is fought on many fronts in Europe. The best known – even in the media of the time – are the western front in France and the eastern front in Russia. The southern front, where Italy and Austria-Hungary face one another, attracts little interest. So during the sixth Battle of the Isonzo, there is only one foreign correspondent, Julius M. Price.

"Some fears were expressed at the time that the hasty withdrawal of the Austrians was a ruse, and that the Italians might find themselves in a fix later on, but, as was soon proved, this was not the case, and nearly the whole of the province of Friuli, that the Austrians had held since 1866, had been redeemed with no opposition worthy of the name, and the Italian front extended from Tolmino to the sea. I was in Cormons shortly after the entry of the troops, and it was difficult to realize that the Italians had not always been there. The inhabitants of Italian origin helped to remove as many traces as possible of the Austrian occupancy — the hated names disappeared as if by magic from shop fronts and street corners; in fact, in a very few hours it was an Italian town again, and the good folk of Cormons had cast off their hated thraldom."

Julius M. Price, British war correspondent in Italy

Germany, c. 1916. Gunroom at the Saalburg Camp. Comradeship acquires a completely new meaning for the soldiers stationed in the trenches. They all share the fate of a daily battle for survival – and help each other as best they can.

"I set my cap down next to me with a pile of cigars in it. I light one. Five metres to my left one of the smallest and cheekiest Berlin recruits, thumped him once on the Yser, couldn't stop winding me up, I can see that he's shaking. I'm piling hand grenades up in front of me. Just in case. The Berliner peers over and, lo and behold, he's following my example: piling up hand grenades, lighting a cigar. (As tranquillizer.) Doesn't take long, all the helmeted men are smoking as far as I can see: five men on my left, ten on my right."

Gerrit Engelke, German soldier, during the Battle of the Somme

Germany, c. 1916.
The everyday life of soldiers, like that of prisoners of war, is characterized by monotony: any distraction is welcome. Bands offer the chance of escaping the monotony or the hell of the trenches for a short time.

"The band has made great strides. I'm now first violin and leader of the orchestra. We have five violins, two cellos and a double bass, besides the drums, two clarinets, flute and banjo, and the Human Crotchet has made commendable progress in writing our music from bits of anything we got through the post, piano solos, and many we have had to write from memory. We perform on Saturday evenings, alternately at either house. Sometimes we sound almost like a seaside band at Home!!! I long for the old Queen's Hall concerts again."

Edward Mousley, 1 May 1917

Italy, 1917. While the German army on the western front has its logistics for transporting both men and vital provisions under firm control in the form of a mature rail network, on the eastern front, marching is often the only means of locomotion and supply.

"*There we rested for a while and then marched back into the town where we were before. Then we came back through a village from where the Russians fired artillery at us, and where we had to pass through at a walking pace, some comrades being wounded. The little houses where we were billeted were also set on fire by the enemy. Another day passed like that. And at night we had to march up a high mountain and carry ammunition crates weighing 100 kg up it. If you can imagine what that means, full uniform, crates like that, when you're wiped out and exhausted, is no small matter. At last we got to the trenches.*"

Karl Kasser, Austrian soldier

France, c. 1915.
The war was supposed to be over by Christmas 1914. In fact, another three Christmases will be celebrated in the trenches before there is, once more, peace in Europe.

"*Christmas was more than meagre, it was primitive – I've had neither a card nor a letter nor a parcel from home. Every day here is just bleakness all around the clock. Inward reflection or even inspiration to write poetry (which our friends the war poets at home do so brilliantly and playfully by the stove at home) is quite impossible. Our only drugs against the revolting void are tobacco and sleep. Rum has been closed off to us for a long time, as there are always some who can't 'moderate themselves'. Even here we're supposed to moderate ourselves!! At least if we could get intoxicated from time to time – not to excess, of course, but decently.*"

Gerrit Engelke, German worker poet and soldier

◀ **Germany, before the war.** A third of the German military budget is spent on the navy. But the fleet is almost entirely insignificant in the war, as a defeat against the still-superior Royal Navy would be disastrous. This leaves only one thing for the sailors on board the port-bound ships in the war: boredom.

"I wanted to set up a nail picture, as all towns and associations were doing. I sketched out a drawing on the board. A mine, peeping from the water, showed a cheerful face. On the horizon you could see our pinnace and the pontoons. Above it were written the words 'Gute Mine zum bösen Spiel'. The lines and surfaces of this picture were to be made entirely out of nails. Firstly: big ten-pfennig nails only for sale to non-commissioned officers; the proceeds for the pub. Secondly: small nails for everyone at a price of five pfennigs for the benefit of blinded fighters. At first the others mocked and annoyed me. But soon people started liking the idea. Petty people like Burkert, Blau and Eckmann refused to pay anything, and spoiled my fun with their carping and grousing, so that in the end I abandoned the plan, paid back all the money I'd collected and decided just to finish the nail picture for my own amusement."

Joachim Ringelnatz, German sailor and author

Saal, France, c. 1915. Really fresh meat becomes an increasing rarity in the German trenches. Only when units organize a slaughtering party, as here in the occupied part of France, is there really enough for everybody.

"Plucked geese and turkeys appeared in large numbers, suspended from the ceilings of billets, and several large barrels arrived on the scene, and were duly placed under lock and key in the canteen, awaiting the auspicious day. Much competition took place between batteries for the possession of the only two live pigs in the village, which eventually went to the highest bidders, while the remainder procured their joints in the form of pork from Doullens. One of the batteries meanwhile grew so attached to its prospective Christmas fare that it was almost decided to spare his life and adopt him as a mascot. His fate was sealed, however, when one day it was discovered that he had disposed of several parcels of food which had, inadvertently, been placed within his reach by some of the men."

C.A. Rose, British soldier

Montmedy, France, c. 1915. Any distraction is welcome in the monotonous everyday life of soldiers in the trenches. The soldiers are particularly proud if they are mentioned in army dispatches.

▶ **Provenchères, France, c. 1915.** While the German offensive in northern France and, above all, in Belgium has achieved great gains in territory, the troops are just behind the French border between Alsace and the Vosges. The enemy seldom seems as close as he is here, where the observation posts in the mountains can be seen from the trenches.

"By car, with Lance-Corporal Bonafoux, to… Boiry Becquerelle, our last village eastwards here. No trench, soldier, or line visible from here, but Henin-sur-Cojeul, in German hands, visible a mile away to the N.E. One of our snipers busy a few hundred yards to the N. We walk E.S.E. through a washed garden of yews, box-edging, and fruit-trees, and beyond, in a corner of an orchard behind a hedge, I am challenged by a corporal in command of a sentry group of two men. I ask him where is our front line. He says, 'Well, Sir, I'm our most advanced post here. We had one up the road on the right, but it was scuppered the other night.'"

C.E. Montague, British war correspondent

"I put colonel through to general or to commander or, indeed, to captain, if these officers are in trenches first, second, third lines or even reserves.

At rest we connect the four regulars plus artillery to the general because we have plenty to do, whether firing or at rest.

I am all the happier for having been 'carried' (mentioned in despatches) because telephone operators are mentioned only rarely in the end. Waiting for the pleasure of being near you two as well as everyone else. Big warm kisses from all my heart."

Maurice Aupetit, French soldier

Montmedy, France, c. 1915. However much the countries of Europe might want a war in 1914, there is a lack of a plan about what it is in fact supposed to achieve. Germany wants 'a place in the sun', Russia wants to avert crisis and revolution, Britain wants to maintain its naval superiority. Only France has a concrete strategic goal – the reconquest of Alsace-Lorraine, fought over for centuries between the two countries. And what's Germany doing in France?

"The defeat of France is the only stage through which we can attain new maritime status, global trade and colonial possessions. Only then can England too be beaten, and European colonization be carried out on our borders."

Hans von Haeften, German general staff

Italy, c. 1916. Old uniforms are disinfected in this huge formalin container. That is urgently necessary, because lice and other vermin have conquered the trenches on both sides.

"Our guns are halfway up the hill outside Pont à Mousson. We arrive in the morning, laden with coffee pots and bread for the team, the soldiers are sitting outside the dugouts, stripped to the waist, shirts spread on their knees, cracking the lice that have taken nest in the stitches."

Ernst Toller, German soldier

Belgium, c. 1915.
An observation post in the trench. In the destructive world of the First World War, bravery plays only a subordinate, passive role. Death has become anonymous, and can strike at any time without warning. The individual soldier can do nothing to increase his chances of survival.

"Let us continue to arm ourselves with courage, do not let us even speak of patience. Nothing but to accept the present moment with all the treasures which it brings us. That is all there is to do, and it is precisely in this that all the beauty of the world is concentrated. There is something, dear mother, something outside all that we have habitually felt. Apply your courage and your love of me to uncovering this, and laying it bare for others."

Anonymous French soldier

Belgium, c. 1915.
Feared as poison gas and machine guns might be, the artillery is by far the deadliest weapon in the war. Guns constantly become bigger and heavier – like the railway gun 'Big Bertha', with a calibre of 42 cm. As artillery fires indirectly – the soldiers don't see their target, but follow instructions about where they are to fire – it can't tell friend from foe, soldier from civilian.

"*We pushed on rapidly through that charnel house, for the stench was fearful, till we stumbled across a sunken road. Here the retreating Germans had evidently made a last desperate stand, but had been caught by our artillery fire. The dead lay in piles, the blue-grey uniforms broken by many a khaki-clad body. I saw the ruins of what was evidently the dressing station, judging by the number of bandaged men about; but a shell had found them out even here and swept them all into the net of death.*"

Father William Doyle, chaplain with the 16th (Irish) Division

Belgium, c. 1915. Even those who have survived the hell of the trenches are in most cases not the same as before. Eventually every soldier breaks when thousands of grenades explode above him and there's nothing, nothing at all, that he can do about it. Back in the civilian world of home – whether on leave or after the war – many soldiers go on carrying their fear around with them. Life will never again be as it once was.

"*I can tell a story of a patrol that disrupted the monotony of our time in the trenches. This concerned the investigation of a deep crater between our line and the enemy line, for whether it was occupied by the enemy. We set off shortly after ten. Artillery and machine guns had already agreed not to fire. So peace prevailed, the English fired off a rifle grenade every now and again. We quickly swing over the sandbag wall, work our way quickly through the wire obstacle, then on our bellies to the crater. Here and there a short pause, when flares came. In a few minutes we had reached the mounds, crept carefully to the edge of the crater, lay there for quite a long time and watched. No sign of the English, but they had left clear traces of visits. Content with this negative result we set off and got back unharmed and undiscovered. We assume that the English use the early morning to make their visits – we choose the evening, and so we stay far away from each other!*"

Fritz Niebergall, German soldier

France, c. 1915. General Joseph Joffre, a veteran of the war of 1870–71 is the commander-in-chief of the French army at the beginning of the war. His appointment is contentious, because he has never commanded an army before.

"The holidays are approaching; my God how I wish they had gone, and how sad those days are going to seem to me. In the end we all need a lot of courage and to ask our Good Lord to cut short this painful ordeal. None the less we cannot count on our regiment retreating. A number of our notable voters, having spoken to their deputies to that effect (what imbeciles), General Joffre added a note to the report saying that in future these breaches of discipline would be severely punished (in good time, luckily our fifteen thousand have no say in the matter) and that the 15th must be very proud of the position of honour he had been given to maintain contact with the enemy for over four months. I have never had any illusions on this matter, and I am very happy about it."

Alexandre Jacqueau, French soldier

Western front, c. 1917. No soldier can survive for long in the trenches, so the units are constantly rotating between the front and the hinterland – where they are ready to react to a possible enemy attack.

"My dear, beloved wife!
At last we are, in line with our captain's 'heart's desire', having to live in the trench. Because he has threatened that so often, we know very well that we owe it to him alone. We were immediately received 'very well'. The shells and shrapnel mostly exploded right in our vicinity. Various bits of iron flew into the trenches, and it's mostly by chance that we weren't hit."

Robert Pöhland, German soldier, to his wife

Italian Alps, c. 1916. The mountain war between Italy and Austria-Hungary stagnates shortly after Italy enters the war. The consequence? Even here in the mountains, trenches are dug.

"The firing line we were making for was in the sector comprised between the Stelvio Pass and the Lake of Garda. In the valley of Guidicaria we reached the trenches, and had our first impression of the magnitude of the operations the Italians are undertaking. What had been accomplished here during the three months since the war started was in evidence before our eyes. I was fully prepared from what I had seen on the Udine front for something equally astonishing in this sector, but I must confess the scenes before me, now that we were in touch with the troops, filled me with amazement. The achievements on the middle Isonzo were great, but here they were little short of the miraculous. It was almost unbelieveable that what we saw was only the work of three short months. Trenches and gun-emplacements confronted you on all sides."

Julius M. Price, British war correspondent in Italy

Germany, c. 1915.
No food, no fighting! Every army depends on a good food supply. On the western front, with its static fronts, supplies are relatively straightforward. On the eastern front, on the other hand, where the enemy armies constantly have to advance or retreat, supplies often don't get through.

"Then one had to go spying again with rifle and bayonet, to observe the enemy. Then it was back to the supply train, again at night, with rifle and bayonet, in a blaze of gunfire, because it was always the enemy's custom to fire even at night. So I was happy to go to the supply station, because you sometimes get something from the cooks there, or from the supply officer, and then it's easier to forget the danger when hunger forces you to. So I once walked the two-hour journey there with all my equipment, back to the supply unit. Turned up there and got coffee from the cook and half a braided loaf."

Karl Kasser, Austrian soldier

Austria, during the war. The army of Austria-Hungary is best-known before the war for its pomp. Colourful uniforms, aigrettes, the most beautiful horses. But the army is not prepared for a modern war. A well-known slogan of the times says: 'We had such a beautiful army, the most beautiful army in the world! And what did they do with that army? They sent it into war.'

▶ **Caricatures in a destroyed house in Wytschaete, Flanders.** The war is the central event in the lives of millions of soldiers and those who stayed behind. The artists among them – like Otto Dix, John Nash, Marc Chagall and Käthe Kollwitz – express their impressions in works that are often just as dark and oppressive as the experience of war itself. Even among the active soldiers, many attempt to get through the eternal waiting by carving or drawing.

"The order came in at 12 o'clock noon that we were going to charge at two. The shooting stopped and we prepared. At exactly two o'clock the call came to 'charge'. When the Russians saw us coming out of the trenches, the shooting really got going. We could only advance sporadically. It was impossible to go more than ten paces. Then you had to dig yourself a shelter again. We advanced like that to the village that had been set alight by the Russians the previous day. There we gathered behind the houses until everyone was together, apart from those who were dead or injured. Then we were to go up to the front and charge. Now, at the word 'fire', we had to go up the mountain. Then there was another river in between that we had to cross. The Russians were still firing. After we'd waded through the river, the water coming up to our chests, we were to go back up the hill on the instruction 'fire'. The Russians were firing less and less, and when we got to the top we saw and heard nothing more. They retreated, leaving only the dead and wounded behind. So it was easy for us to charge the mountain."

Karl Kasser, Austrian soldier

"The danger for the artist in the war will be that the sensitivity of his soul (silver bromide plate, then subjected to strenuous development) will be dulled, that the main nerve of his sensibility will be numbed by the violence and horror of the events that he has endured for years. What is a storm for him now, at which he once marvelled, which he once greeted as the most powerful natural event, compared to the barrage of tear gas grenades? He will probably have to get used to forgetting the noisiest things and those most terrible to the eye, that he may harmonize once more in the gentle, ebbing pulse of the rhythm of the patches of green, the undulating landscape and the rising forests, and the more violently raging storm of the cities – will have to forget in order to rejoice and be able, joyfully, to create."

Gerrit Engelke, German worker poet and soldier

THE TERROR

"How far he had walked, we could not guess; at the time of our meeting, he was crawling along the ground and – what with the blood and the mud on him – scarcely looked human at all."

Marina Yurlova, Russian Cossack soldier
fighting in Armenia

At the beginning of the war, every country involved in the conflict maintained the conviction that they were engaged in defensive warfare. For the first few years, there were very few pacifists in the countries involved in the war – and those individuals had little influence on public opinion. As time went on, sanctions were introduced even in constitutional states such as Britain, France, Germany and Austria-Hungary, particularly with regard to compulsory labour in the armament industry. Given that the trades unions received participation rights at the same time, the regulations were met with little resistance. Only in Russia did the ruling powers react violently to food riots and strikes that arose everywhere during the course of the war. But the military administrations in occupied zones and behind the front lines did turn to brutal measures. The German, Austro-Hungarian and Russian militaries in particular contravened human rights and international treaties.

German soldiers outside their dugout on the eastern front. The longer the war lasts, the more fallen men have to be replaced – often by raw recruits.

In neutral Belgium, the country's regular troops were quickly pushed back by the Germans and the Belgian strongholds swiftly conquered. The Germans were especially fearful of the *franc-tireurs*, guerilla fighters, who

Seriously wounded Austrian soldiers being loaded onto a horse-drawn cart at the eastern front. Whether they survive the difficult journey to the field hospital is uncertain.

would lie in wait for troop units, carrying out attacks on railway lines and at railway stations. The German military responded with terror. Hostages were taken in the occupied zones, and more than 5,500 civilians were shot as a deterrent or as 'retribution'. In 1916, 120,000 Belgians were deported to Germany for forced labour.

In Leuven in the Belgian region of Flanders, German troops perpetrated a massacre after a night-time exchange of fire. The German military leaders ordered that an example be made, and 209 people were shot in their homes. The city's 42,000 inhabitants were driven out and almost 1,100 houses burned. Even the famous library at the Catholic University in Leuven was set on fire, leading to the destruction of thousands of medieval manuscripts and incunabula. In total, 230,000 books fell victim to the flames. According to Article 247 of the Peace Treaty of Versailles, an equivalent number of manuscripts, incunabula and books had to be sent from Germany after the war.

Even more horrific was the behaviour of German troops towards the inhabitants of the little town of Dinant in the Wallonian part of Belgium. On 23 August 1914 hostages were shot under the pretext of needing to advance against the resistance movement. One-fifth of the population, some 612 people, were killed, including 92 women and seven babies. Almost 1,300 of 1,800 houses were burnt to the ground. There were further massacres in August 1914 in Aarschot (Flanders), resulting in 156 deaths, in Andenne (Wallonia) with 211 and in Tamines (Wallonia) with 384 victims. With war crimes like these, Germany gained a bad reputation at the very start of the war in most of the neutral countries. The attempts to justify their actions made the issue even worse, for example the protestation of the Bavarian Higher Regional Court Judge and Reichstag representative Ernst Müller-Meiningen. He claimed that the hostage-taking and shootings were carried out to protect German soldiers and therefore 'a direct safeguarding of international law and humanity'.

Galician refugees by a railway line. When Russian troops occupy Galicia, which belongs to Austria-Hungary in autumn 1914, millions of inhabitants flee their homes.

In August 1915, English nurse Edith Cavell was imprisoned for having helped Allied prisoners-of-war to flee into the neutral Netherlands. She was subsequently court-martialled, sentenced to death and shot on 15 October 1915, together with the Belgian architect Philippe Baucq, who had led the escape. The other 26 members of the group were either given lesser sentences or granted a reprieve. Senior physician and poet Dr Gottfried Benn was present in court and at the execution, and later wrote a report on the proceedings. His account of the nurse's execution led to protests all over the world. In the English-speaking world, Edith Cavell became a martyr of a cruel occupying regime which ignored both the rules of international law and the honour code. Even today, an annual memorial service is held at her grave in Norwich. After the extreme reaction from the rest of the world, the German government ordered that women no longer be executed. Despite this, Belgian woman Elise Grandprez was executed in 1917 after being found guilty of spying. Alongside Edith Cavell, she was the second martyr of the Belgian resistance.

The employment of forced labour on the front was also part of the darker side of warfare. The French army had started to use forced labour in 1916. By the end of the same year, up to 20,000 French prisoners of war were forced to work on the German side of the front at Verdun, and in such a way that they could be clearly seen by their French comrades. These measures, which were illegal according to the law of war, were brought to the public's attention through the European press. The matter was discussed in the parliaments of Berlin and Paris. Eventually, the French government ordered that prisoners of war be taken from the front and relocated to other areas of the country. After this, the Germans pulled back their forced labourers.

While attention was focused on the mistreatment of prisoners of war in Verdun, it went unnoticed that the Germans were preparing a partial retreat on the Somme, destroying in the process an area spanning thirty by a hundred kilometres. The population, more than 125,000 people, were deported. Seventy thousand workers were put to work on the new fortifications, half of whom were French, Belgian and Russian forced labourers and the other half German contract workers. Many died due to insufficient food supplies and lack of warm clothing; not just forced labourers, but German workers too. For this reason, many of the latter left the sites, leaving almost only forced labourers. General Erich Ludendorff, the general quartermaster of the supreme army command, later concluded from these experiences that 'forced labour was an indispensable component of successful modern warfare'.

The prisoner-of-war camp of Strzałkowo, which was built by Russian prisoners of war. How many of the prisoners interned here failed to survive is not documented.

In the east, the violence was often aimed at the local population. Attempts to acquire connections and business partners through the fronts was declared to be espionage by the Austrian and Russian military, and became punishable by death. The Jews, in particular, were especially vulnerable to persecution by Russian soldiers. *Der Bund*, the organization of the Jewish proletariat in Russia, reported in the French newspaper *L'Humanité* about atrocities and pogroms from Lódz in Russian Poland to Bukovina.

One of the most horrific crimes was the genocide of more than one million Armenians carried out by the Ottoman Empire. The Turkish authorities accused them of having helped the Russian troops during the winter offensive of 1914/15 in the Armenian highlands. The German Orientalist Johannes Lepsius, who formed a support organization for the Armenians, declared the accusations to be unsustainable and fabricated. The Armenian population was alleged to have been deported from the highlands to Deir es Sor in Mesopotamia, a place much too small to

The graves of four soldiers from the Battle of Tannenberg. Many soldiers do not find their eternal rest in decorated graves, but in the countless mass graves that line the battlefields on every front.

(*Opposite*) German soldiers in the ruined church of Warneton, Belgium. Fuhrmann's description of the photograph refers explicitly to the fact that the church was shot to pieces by the British.

accommodate hundreds of people, let alone millions. It had never been the Turkish government's intention that the deportees would reach their destination.

Unlike the war crimes committed against the inhabitants of the occupied zones, the merciless military justice of all the states may have been justified in terms of international law, but it was still questionable by constitutional standards. This served more as a deterrent than a punishment. Even the British soldiers who signed up voluntarily at the beginning of the war were subjected to this. The twenty-year-old soldier George Ward was among the first of those to be 'made an example of'. Shocked by the severe injuries of two of his comrades, he reported himself as sick without having actually been wounded. In his file is a comment by the commander-in-chief, General Sir Douglas Haig: 'It is necessary to make an example to prevent cowardice in the face of the enemy as far as possible.' Ward received the death sentence and was shot dead, just like 271 other British soldiers, 750 Italian, 75 French and 48 German. Many military judges ruled less severely, taking into account that the accused were still in shock from the trenches. An attempt by peace activists in Great Britain to attain a posthumous amnesty for all the executed failed in 1993, rejected by John Major's government.

August Fuhrmann's photographs avoid the horrors of the front. Superficially, there are few images in the collection that deal with atrocities of war – mainly mass graves and burials. But if we look more closely, we discover pictures that – willingly or not – reflect the true nature of the conflict.

Muschaken, East Prussia, 1915. Although many aspects of the First World War are modern, new and technologically up-to-date, the use of animals remains important. Many millions of horses and mules serve as mounts and pack animals, many hundreds of thousands of dogs trace mines, warn against poison gas or, as do thousands of trained carrier pigeons, bring news directly from the fiercely embattled trenches of the front. The death toll among these creatures is, like that of the soldiers, huge. On the German side alone over a million horses die – like these on a battlefield near Muschaken.

"In the horror-zone. The rainy twilight shadows the road, and suddenly, in a ditch – the dead! They have dragged themselves here from the battlefield – they are all corrupt now. The coming of darkness makes it difficult to distinguish their nationality, but the same great pity envelops them all. Only one word for them: poor boy! The night for these ignominies – and then again the morning. The day rises upon the swollen bodies of dead horses. In the corner of a wood, carnage, long cold. One sees only open sacks, ripped nose-bags. Nothing that looks like life remains."

Anonymous French soldier

Serbia, c. 1916. The countless dead of the First World War are mostly buried where they die – in mass graves directly behind the front.

"Terrible bombardment, worse than any man can bear. It is a wonder I am still alive... the sound of artillery is the voice of death. Fear is driving people mad. I too think I am heading that way. Yes, I am shaking with fear and despondency. It is all very well to talk of putting up a fight, but in reality it is not humanly possible. It is enough to drive you insane. Dead, wounded, massive losses. This is the end. Unprecedented slaughter, a horrific bloodbath. There is blood everywhere and the dead and bits of bodies lie scattered about so that..."

The last entry of an anonymous Austrian officer whose diary was found on the battlefield after his death

Western front, during the war. Between the trenches lies no-man's-land. Blasted by countless thousands of grenades, it is like a lunar landscape in which nothing can grow or flourish. The phrase no-man's-land is coined by the English soldier and historian Ernest Swinton. The trauma of no-man's-land is so great that the English term even finds its way into the French language.

"'Keep your nappers down, you rooks. Don't look over the top. It ayen't 'ealthy.' It is the regular warning to new men. For some reason the first emotion of the rookie is an overpowering curiosity. He wants to take a peep into no-man's-land. It feels safe enough when things are quiet. But there's always a Fritzie over yonder with a telescope-sighted rifle, and it's about ten to one he'll get you if you stick the old 'napper' up in daylight."

R. Derby Holmes, American volunteer in the British Army

Eastern Prussia, 1915. View of a Russian mass grave on the eastern front. Pictures such as this from the First World War are extremely rare. It contradicts the myth of the heroic soldier too violently. But for the men at the front, living with death is an everyday situation.

"This place is half burned out and in a terrible state; the inhabitants proved very hostile yesterday and were severely punished for it. Many poor innocent people had to suffer! This kind of warfare, forced on us by criminal fools, is shocking. If only people would accept the way of reason."

Lieutenant Colonel Hans von Beseler (1850–1921) in a letter of 20 August 1914 from Aarschot, where 119 inhabitants were shot

"On Sunday I drove out to Pervyse with a kind friend, Mr Tapp. At the end of the long avenue by which one approaches the village, Pervyse church stands, like a sentinel with both eyes shot out. Nothing is left but a blind stare. Hardly any of the church remains, and the churchyard is as if some devil had stalked through it, tearing up crosses and kicking down graves. Even the dead are not left undisturbed in this awful war. The village (like many other villages) is just a mass of gaping ruins – roofs blown off, streets full of holes, not a window left unshattered, and the guns still booming."

Sarah Macnaughtan, Scottish volunteer nurse

Tannenberg, Eastern Prussia, 1915. So-called 'heroes' mass graves' near Tannenberg. More than 3,000 Germans and 30,000 Russians fell during this battle early in the war. Their graves are supposed to be seen as a symbol of victory – but the more such mass graves there are on all fronts, the less the soldiers believe in this cult of the dead.

Peronne, France, 1914. While the politicians of the belligerent countries promise a short, almost bloodless war and a glorious victory, most servicemen sense that, with the modern weapons at their disposal, neither is possible.

"Once you have seen these graves by the roadside going east, you will hardly go a mile in two hundred which has not its graves. From the environs of Meaux, a scant twenty miles from Paris, to the frontier at the Seille, there are graves and more graves, where men fought hand to hand. Passing them in a swift-moving auto, they seem to march by you; there is the illusion of an army advancing on the hillside, until at last, beyond Nancy, you come to the great common graves, and you read 'Here rest 179 French soldiers', or across the road, 'Here 196 Germans'."

Frank Herbert Simonds, American author and journalist

"Oh; I forgot to say, about the tragic side of war – 'war as it is', etc – that in all the horrors I've seen at one time or another there was nothing that did not fall within what I had always expected. To see carnage isn't a revelation at all – it's only a verification; and my previous detestation of war in general, and my idea of it as a thing to be always avoided by all honourable means, is exactly the feeling that I shall come away with at the end of this war."

C.E. Montague, British war correspondent

Illowo, Eastern Prussia, c. 1915. The grave of a Cossack who fell during the invasion of Eastern Prussia. The Cossacks are the Tsar's elite warriors. A tradition several centuries old makes the warlike riders into feared fighters who will willingly die for their Tsar.

"I realized that Kosel had been shielding me with his body, for when he moved aside I saw for the first time what we had to face; directly in front lay the great concrete bridge, and beyond it was a wall of men, moving down the mountainside, firing as they came on. Kosel gave me a smile of extraordinary sweetness, and half rose to his feet. It was a desperate thing to do, and in that very moment I saw the shapka torn from his head. There was a sound I shall never forget and could not describe even if I would. Kosel plunged forward, blood spouting like a fountain from his forehead, blood on the grass. He half rolled over and lay still, his beard red and dripping."

Marina Yurlova, Russian Cossack soldier

Luigi Cadorna, Italian commander-in-chief, at the start of the war. Italy – before the war still an ally of Germany and Austria-Hungary – is lured into the war by promises made by the Entente powers. But many Italian soldiers are correspondingly unwilling. To inspire them to fight, the Italian commander-in-chief Luigi Cadorna gives orders that those units which refuse to attack are to be 'decimated' – every tenth soldier, whether guilty or not, is to be shot.

"'Trieste o morte!' I saw chalked upon the walls all over north Italy. That is the Italian objective. And they are excellently led. Cadorna is an old Roman, a man cast in the big simple mould of antiquity, frugal in his tastes, clear in his aims, with no thought outside his duty."

Arthur Conan Doyle, British author

A funeral in Romania, before the war.

Within a very short time the war destroys the achievements of centuries. Diseases which, though not eradicated before the war, but which had been forced back by advances in medicine and hygiene, return with unprecedented ferocity.

"The heat came, heavy, oppressive. People died like flies. Dysentery raged. The road past our house, that road which led to East Prussia, led also to the cemetery – little no longer – no longer peaceful. There was one constant stream of peasant funerals, with now and then a more pretentious one with the priest. It was a common sight to see people carrying a rough box, with a bit of green upon it, or all wrapped up in a shawl, singing the song for the dead as they slowly and painfully went on their way. The wail of those voices still rings in my ears – supremely melancholy and hopeless. Hopeless for themselves – for the dead were rather to be envied. War had taken the sting away! Often I saw them resting by the roadside, saying prayers for the dead that the time be not lost, then going on till they reached the cemetery – where they must dig the grave. Hours after those people had passed, on their way to the cemetery, we would see them returning, the cross-bearer going on before. That cross! Often it was only two pieces of wood bound together – there were not enough crosses in the church to serve the increasing number of funerals – and yet there had to be a cross."

Laura de Gozdawa Turczynowicz, American woman living in occupied Russian Poland

Reims, France, 1914. For the first time in history, millions of prisoners of war fall into enemy hands for years. Plans for dealing with them did not exist before the First World War. Diseases rage in the overcrowded camps – and leave as many dead as the combat in the battlefields.

"For all my misfortune, I was lucky to be able to leave hospital after fourteen days. I ended up in a cholera ward, in fact. There were twenty of us men in the room. Most of them Russians and Chinese, and some prisoners were there too, and I couldn't talk to them either. Some of them died terrible deaths while I was lying in the room. They tossed and turned in a fever until they were dead and heat issued from their mouths and noses. It was a sorry sight, and one thought one would soon be finished too."

Karl Kasser, Austrian soldier

▶ **France, c. 1916.** A monument to French children killed near the front by French artillery shells. For German propaganda, such events are manna from heaven, and can be used to whip up support for the war – much in the way that their opponents use news of civilians killed by German Zeppelins. That many more thousands of children die of hunger and illness goes unmentioned.

"The children were so near death that day that I went from one to the other, changing compresses, wetting the lips with weak tea (made of melted snow water – the wells were not possible), imploring them not to leave me. One of the new officers told me there was a celebrated doctor in Suwalki that day. Did I not wish to see him? How I blessed the man for his thought. In a short time the doctor came. Of course he only looked at the children when he said: 'Typhus' – and one near the crisis, that very soon the finger would have to be operated upon, also that the military could not be quartered in the house. I would at least be alone. The nurse, Stephania, had never come back after the secret police got after her, so that day I called Jacob's daughter, Manya, into service in the sick room."

Laura de Gozdawa Turczynowicz, American woman living in occupied Russian Poland

◄ Gluci, Serbia, c. 1916. In the war-torn areas of Belgium, stray shells are still found well into the future. But it will be many more decades before the battlefields of Serbia are cleared of the traces of death and destruction.

"I wake before day. I walk through the village, past the black burned walls of gunned-out houses, I fall into the shell-holes that churn up the streets. The door of a church stands open. I go in, the day falls grey through the shattered panes, my heavy boots echo on the tiles of the stone floor. A soldier lies before the altar. As I bend over him I see that he's dead. His head is broken open in the middle, the halves gape apart like an enormous egg shell, the brain spills out like pulp."

Ernst Toller, German soldier and poet

East Prussia, c. 1915. Above all, the state of Austria-Hungary, which incorporates many different peoples, has great problems stirring the soldiers to fight for the German-Hungarian upper class. Many soldiers of Slavic origins sympathize with their Russian and Serbian enemies. Draconian punishments are introduced to halt the desertions.

"Military crimes
Anyone will be summarily shot who:
1) Abandons his troop out of cowardice. Guilty of this crime will be anyone who:
  a) Is found behind his troops or in the hinterland without the required and stamped authorization.
  b) Stays with the supply train without justification.
  c) Goes to a paramedical station when uninjured or insignificantly injured.
2) Who retreats from the front line without being ordered to do so.
3) Who does not immediately stop during a retreat, when ordered to do so.
4) Who surrenders without extreme resistance.
5) Who discards weapons or ammunition or abandons guns, ammunition cars and horses in a cowardly fashion and abandons them to the enemy.
6) Who harms himself.
7) Who speaks timidly (prompting cowardice by exaggerating the strength of the enemy and his successes).
Desertion to the enemy is punished as the most shameful crime with death by hanging."

Order of the Austro-Hungarian fighting forces, 12 February 1915

Aleppo, Ottoman Empire, c. 1916. The victims of this war are not only those who die in the huge battles of attrition, like those of the Somme, Verdun or Erzerum. Seven million civilians die of hunger, siege – and in the first genocide in history – mass murder of the Armenians.

"Mr Hills and Dr Gordon (American missionaries) seem to think they would like me to join them in their work for the Armenians. These unfortunate people have been nearly exterminated by massacres, and it has been officially stated that 75 per cent of the whole race has been put to the sword. This sounds awful enough, but when we consider that there is no refinement of torture that has not been practised upon them, then something within one gets up and shouts for revenge. The photographs which General Bernoff has are proof of the devildom of the Turks, only that the devil could not have been so beastly, and a beast could not have been so devilish."

Sarah Macnaughtan, Scottish nurse in Russia

Armenia, September 1915. From the point of view of the Ottoman supreme commanders, the Christian Armenians represent an immediate danger in the country – they would collaborate with the Russians, also Christian. In order to prevent this, 1.5 million Armenians are 'forcibly resettled'. In reality, this means their death sentence.

"Realizing that the clouds of dust we were raising must necessarily attract the attention of enemy planes, I commented as such to Estad Bey so that he would change the formation. But he, confiding in God knows what, merely smiled at my fears, which he considered excessive and, when he arrived, had the regiments drawn up in close formation all along the swamp, without even giving precautionary orders. The result of this oversight, inexcusable in a divisional commander, was as could only be expected. When we dismounted, as if by magic six or seven enemy planes appeared which, before we even had time to sound the alarm, rained bombs down on us that in less than half a minute perhaps caused more casualties than the fire from their infantry and artillery the previous day. Almost two hundred horses lay dying on the ground or fled in panic, pouring blood or with their intestines hanging out, in every direction, dragging their riders by the stirrups or trampling on anyone trying to restrain them."

Rafael de Nogales, Venezuelan volunteer in the Ottoman Army

Armenia, during the genocide. There were attacks on Christian Armenians decades before the First World War. As early as 1896 organized gangs – tolerated by the Ottoman authorities – kill over 10,000 Armenians in Istanbul, after Armenian separatists had taken hostages in a bank in order to achieve independence.

"I remember the first time I ever saw one of these, on his return. I was out with my Hundred, riding somewhere beyond the last camp, when we came across him. He had not been treated very hospitably; no doubt there was a food shortage among our enemies too. This one had had his left eye burned out. His right hand had been chopped off at the wrist. They had slit his tongue. How far he had walked, we could not guess; at the time of our meeting, he was crawling along the ground and – what with the blood and the mud on him – scarcely looked human at all."

Marina Yurlova, Russian Cossack soldier fighting in Armenia

Enver Pasha, during the war. As War Minister, Enver Pasha is de facto the supreme commander and the most powerful man in the Ottoman Empire – and one of those chiefly responsible for the Armenian genocide.

"The feeling of momentary calm that charming sight inspired in my tormented mind was brusquely interrupted by the atrocious spectacle offered by a hill alongside the track that was crowned with thousands of half-naked, bloody bodies heaped on top of each other or entwined in the final embrace of death. Fathers, brothers, sons and grandsons lay there as they had fallen under the bullets and scimitars of their assassins. The trembling limbs of the dying protruded from more than one of these piles of bodies. Life escaped in gushes of warm blood from more than one slit throat. Everywhere, flocks of crows picked at the eyes of the dead and dying, who in their fixed stares seemed still to reflect all the horrors of an indescribable agony, while carrion dogs sank their sharp fangs into the entrails of beings where the force of life was still beating."

Rafael de Nogales, Venezuelan volunteer in the Ottoman Army

Istanbul, before the war. The genocide of the Armenians occurs in full view of the public. Even the German allies know about the extent and goal of the 'resettlements'. Again and again employees of the German ambassador in Istanbul try to persuade the German government to do something about it.

"In our press we should also express our displeasure with the persecution of the Armenians and stop praising the Turks to the skies. What they are doing is our work, they are our officers, our guns, our money. Without our help the overinflated frog will collapse in on itself. We do not need to be so fearful in our treatment of the Turks. They will not easily go over to the other side and make peace. In order to be successful in the Armenian question we will have to make the Turkish government fearful of the consequences. If we do not stand our ground more firmly, we will have no option but to look on with further unsuccessful caveats that are more irritating than they are useful, as our ally continues to perpetuate massacres."

Paul Graf Wolff Metternich, German ambassador in Istanbul, to Reich Chancellor Theobald von Bethmann-Hollweg

Armenia, February 1919. In the end what is more important for the German government is the need to support Turkey. It is strategically vital that Germany preserves this ally rather than avert the massacre of the Armenians with a clumsy intervention.

"The proposed public affronting of an ally in the course of an ongoing war would be a measure hitherto unknown in history. Our only goal is to keep Turkey on our side until the end of the war, whether Armenians perish or not. Should the war last longer, we will have even greater need of the Turks. I don't understand how Metternich can make this suggestion."

Reich Chancellor Theobald von Bethmann-Hollweg

Armenia, during the genocide. The official view of the Ottoman, and later Turkish, authorities is that the Armenian casualties are the consequences of war and resettlement. The extent of the murder is denied even today.

"As we approached the bridge over the Tokma Su, it was certainly a fearful sight. As far as the eye could see over the plain was this slow-moving line of ox carts. For hours there was not a drop of water on the road, and the sun poured down its very hottest. As we went on we began to see the dead from yesterday's company, and the weak began to fall by the way. The Kurds working in the fields made attacks continually, and we were half-distracted. I piled as many as I could on our wagons, and our pupils, both boys and girls, worked like heroes. One girl took a baby from its dead mother and carried it until evening. Another carried a dying woman until she died. We bought water from the Kurds, not minding the beating that the boys were sure to get with it. I counted forty-nine deaths, but there must have been many more. One naked body of a woman was covered with bruises. I saw the Kurds robbing the bodies of those not yet entirely dead..."

Mary-Louise Graffam, American teacher in Armenia

Dobrenovac, Serbia, c. 1916. Serbia bears the most severe losses in the war in proportion to its population. Fifteen per cent of the population as a whole and twenty-five per cent of Serbian soldiers do not survive the war.

"Along the roadsides and in the hills one came across many a cemetery. Alas, pestilence and war had added so great a number to God's Acres that many an extra field shows its harvest of small wooden crosses – a harvest of men who had passed beyond in the turmoil of battle or gripped by the hand of fever. Whichever the route, these heroes took the journey pro patria. They were in rows, those small wooden crosses – hundreds and hundreds – many to an 'Unknown Soldier'. Somewhere weary hearts were longing for the face that they would never see. The farmer ploughed around the new field which bore its human harvest. No line, no fences stretched in demarcation. By now, perhaps, the furrow of the plough extends to where the bones of the brave lie rotting."

Dr Caroline Matthews, Scottish doctor in Serbia

Gorizia, Italy, 1917. The huge cemeteries of soldiers on all fronts are officially called 'hero cemeteries'. In the Italian cemeteries alone, at the end of the war there are over a million Italian and Austrian soldiers.

"*The spectacle we had before us of violence and death is indescribable. Everything had been levelled and literally pounded to atoms by the Italian artillery. The ground all around was pitted with shell holes, and strewn with every imaginable kind of debris: the remains of barbed-wire entanglements in such chaotic confusion that it was frequently a matter of positive difficulty to pass at all; broken rifles, unused cartridges by the thousand, fragments of shellcases, boots, first-aid bandages, and odds and ends of uniforms covered with blood.*"

Julius M. Price, British war correspondent in Italy

Carpathians, Romania, c. 1916. The grave of cavalry officer Peter Carp. For Elfriede Kuhr, the death of her idol, pilot Werner Waldecker, definitively brings to an end her enthusiasm for the war.

"Dear Diary, I have written a letter to the mother of Lieutenant Werner Waldecker. I have sent the envelope to the residents' registration office of the city of Bielefeld, with a request to pass it on to Frau Waldecker. In the letter I write that she is not alone with her suffering. I loved her son so much because he was such an innocent person. I wrote that I had already written many poems and a story about him. But I didn't write that I have his faded red rose in a black box."

Elfriede Kuhr, German schoolgirl

▶ **Russia, c. 1916.** Apart from the invasion of East Prussia, Germany is spared the direct effects of the war. The people in Serbia, Austria-Hungary, Belgium, Italy, France and Russia are, however, subject to the full onslaught of the war.

"It wasn't until we were about 500–600 metres from the first houses of Montigny that heavy gunfire reached us. I threw myself into the field and madly tried to find shelter behind a little haystack. The men, assuming that the gunfire came from local inhabitants, charged wildly into the village. They saw only human figures fleeing the village for the Chiers Valley. Montigny too was burned down."

Colonel Christoph von Ebbinghaus, commander of (Württemberg) Infantry Regiment 125

"*It is, however, terrible that so many civilians have to be punished because they shoot at our people, that whole villages are being burned and destroyed. It produced horrible, shattering images and experiences.*"

Harry Graf Kessler, German diplomat

Łodž-Zgierz, Russian Poland, c. 1916.
The horrors of war, of the trenches, of the constant possibility of death by chance – the soldiers of the First World War will never shake it off. Shell shock and similar psychological illnesses will mark many of them even years after the war.

"With complete indifference I thought only one thing: this is the final moment before dying. Beside me I was aware of many comrades, as silent as myself, but already completely dead. Only sometimes a horrible cry rose up, I couldn't tell whether it was near or far, then there was groaning or the sound of death-rattles. I also heard scraps of words. When I close my eyes I still hear them just as I did then: 'Quick, you asses, here, grab hold, press! Firmly!' ... 'Yes, Doctor. Now, am I needed?'... 'Not here, but over there, they...'."

Hermann Stehr, German author

Mass graves being dug in Serbia, c. 1916. Medicine has made enormous advances before and during the First World War. Many injuries that would previously have been fatal are suddenly survivable – if they can be treated quickly enough. But infected wounds often mean amputation, and can even lead to death.

"*There: someone's shouting, 'Comrade'. He looks along the limping row. No one moves. For the second time: 'Comrade!' He goes on looking. He sees that on the steps under the altar there lies a bundle, red and blue. The bundle moves, with a very delicate motion a hand rises from it. Reisiger goes closer. A French officer. He is wearing a cap with gold braids. A pale face with a black pointed beard. What now? He understands only a few French phrases, but he will hardly be able to make himself understood. The hand waves again. He takes another step closer. The officer throws open his coat; his uniform coat is unbuttoned, on the dirty shirt there is a big damp bloodstain. The officer's hand points to that stain. It trembled and flutters back and forth. Help? – Reisiger hasn't the courage to lift the shirt and look at the wound. He murmurs a few German words and then goes on tiptoe through the whole church to the exit and calls out, 'Orderlies'.*"

Edlef Köppen, German soldier

Mass graves being dug in Crna Bara, Serbia, c. 1916. Worse than the thought of sudden death by artillery shell is the fear of being wounded during an attack in no-man's-land. Those who fall here must usually be left behind. The chance of survival is low.

"The fire gradually subsides. It gets dark. Now that it's become quiet, in front of and behind us we hear the heartrending cries for help of the injured. Help is impossible. One would get lost on the terrain, and fired on by the rattling machine guns. Our stretcher-bearers are all injured, too. We are all weary to the point of collapse, but we can't think of sleep. All night the cries rise up from the shell holes. They fall silent more and more towards morning. We nod off a little while standing."

Gerrit Engelke, German worker poet and soldier

◀ **East Prussia, Germany, 1915.**
A house destroyed by Russian troops. The invasion of East Prussia by Russian troops lasts barely a month. It is a month full of anxiety in Germany – and propaganda stokes that fear for the rest of the war.

"But yesterday and today there has been nothing but processions of refugees. Grandmother said they wail terribly. 'The Russians nailed a woman to a barn door – like this.' Mariechen stood by the kitchen door with her arms and legs spread wide, making her look like one of the owls that our superstitious peasants nail to the barn doors to ward off lightning. When Mariechen tells horror stories, however true, you can't help laughing. She has a broad, bony, red face and thin, straw-blonde hair. And she lisps."

Elfriede Kuhr, German schoolgirl

France, c. 1916. In many armies, including Germany's, it is the task of the immediate superior officers to inform relatives about the death of a soldier. Almost 10 million soldiers die in the course of the war.

"Dear Frau Gettmann!
I must sadly inform you that your son died a heroic death for the fatherland on 20.6. Your son was shot through the neck and died immediately, he is buried 19 km south of Cowsany station. In the name of the division I wish to convey our warmest sympathy, we are losing, in your son, a dear comrade and an extraordinarily brave and hard-working NCO. I will always be grateful to him for the outstanding services he performed for me. We have taken our revenge on him. 100 Russians have paid the price. Console yourself with the thought that his blood fell for Germany's greatness."

Your servant Captain Haken

Hollebeke, Belgium, c. 1915. According to the Schlieffen Plan, Germany expect that marching through Belgium will be a simple matter. The tireless resistance of the Belgian army leads in the end to the failure of all German military plans. The hatred of the occupying German troops towards the Belgians is further fuelled by the fact that the violation of Belgian neutrality is the official reason for Britain to enter the war.

"The Dutch seem well-disposed towards us, and even bring presents for our people. The behaviour of the Belgians, on the other hand, is unspeakable; they do not reveal themselves as a civilized people, but as a band of robbers; a fine consequence of Belgium being governed by clerics. But we have immediately made our point of view quiet clear, and they will have to see sense. They have been the biggest asses in the world! We wouldn't have touched a hair on their heads, they would have made millions upon millions from our invasion, and probably their country wouldn't even have become a theatre of war. Instead they are rousing the French, setting the English at our throats and laying waste their own country. This miserable hybrid state needs to be removed or so squeezed that the fools in Brussels and Antwerp lose their love of France once and for all."

Colonel-General Hans von Beseler in a letter to his wife

Haelen, Belgium, August 1914. The longer the war goes on, the more normal living with death becomes to the soldiers. They share their trenches with the dead – whether friend or foe.

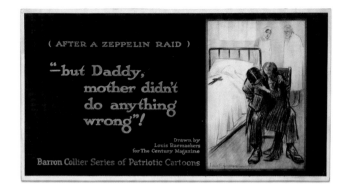

(AFTER A ZEPPELIN RAID)

"-but Daddy, mother didn't do anything wrong"!

Drawn by
Louis Raemaekers
for The Century Magazine

Barron Collier Series of Patriotic Cartoons

Postcard, USA, 1916. The feared German Zeppelins actually do very little damage. But their psychological effect is enormous – and not only to the benefit of the Germans.

"The air here is foul, in the most complete sense of the word, because here in this position that we have just stormed, there are Frenchmen lying around all over the place, filling the air with their perfume, which is not Roger et Gallet, Paris.

Recently during a general gun battle during the night, unfortunately I think I am right in saying that my right eardrum burst. Reporting yourself sick from the front-line trench is difficult, so I will have to wait for the doctor's judgment until we're relieved. My hearing is pretty bad now. But I'm glad if I can hear my beloved music (and will put that to the test when on leave). I'm in a far from gloomy mood."

Gerrit Engelke, German worker poet and soldier

"A frightful lot of harm must have been done by the panic shrieking of the London newspapers about the enemy air raids. If anything could make the Germans more certain to go on with their raiding of England it would be these terrified squeals over a handful of casualties, as casualties go in this war."

C.E. Montague, British war correspondent

THE END

> "The only German we see as we go into Mons is a dead one lying under the boulevard trees. As we go in, the streets are crowded with civilians, cheering and waving flags and shouting English words to us."

C.E. Montague, British war correspondent

German soldiers swear allegiance to their supreme commander, Kaiser Wilhelm II. Many of them will pay for the oath with their lives.

The year 1917 ended with good prospects for the Germans. The October Revolution in Russia seemed to promise the end of the war in the east. The German ruling powers had made a decisive contribution to the Bolshevik victory by bringing Lenin and the entire party leadership from Switzerland to Scandinavia. The German military provided the revolutionaries with more than 20,000 Reichsmark, a sum which equated to 50,000 dollars back then. The Bolshevists repaid the sum, but not until 1923 when, due to hyperinflation, it was worth less than one dollar.

Despite the confidence in the east, the mood amongst the malnourished and exhausted German soldiers worsened. During the transport of troops from the eastern to the western front, ten per cent of the soldiers deserted. On the wagons departing for the west, the slogans no longer said 'To Paris!', but instead 'Cattle for slaughter in Flanders'.

On 21 March, the German troops began Operation Michael on the Somme, pushing forward in the weeks that followed almost to the city of Amiens and the French headquarters in Compiègne. But the Germans arrived at the very area which they themselves had destroyed at the start of 1917. The streets were as desolate and ruined as the streams and brooks. It was like a lunar landscape in which there wasn't even any water. But there were British supply depots, filled with food supplies and alcohol, so the German soldiers refused to advance any further. Allegedly, General Ludendorff was incensed that 'the whole division just ate and drank themselves silly from the looted enemy supplies, and didn't proceed with the attack'. On 4 April, British troops waged a counter-attack, and 'Operation Michael' became a failure. The losses in those four weeks to the German side were 360,000 fallen and wounded. In mid-April, the chief of staff of the 6th Army reported that: 'The troops didn't attack, despite their orders. The offensive was a failure'.

Austro-Hungarian officers in conference on the eastern front. At the start of the war the Austro-Hungarian army is considered the finest in the world.

Ludendorff made one more attempt and managed to advance as far as the Marne, enabling the German troops to fire their most powerful artillery at Paris, which was 120 kilometres away. But then the American divisions stepped in, including the marines, who were renowned for their toughness. In June 1918, the impact of the influenza epidemic which had made its way from South Africa via Spain (hence the name 'Spanish' flu) to western and central Europe became massively evident. By June, half a million German soldiers were ill.

Ludendorff had overexerted the troops with all his offensives. That soon became clear when French and American troops (on 18 July), and British troops (on 8 August) launched a counter-attack with hundreds of tanks. These Allied offensives were, as German secret service chief Walter Nicolai wrote, no surprise. To him, the surprise was the failure of the German troops. France's Marshall Foch 'marched towards a crumbling German front'.

The American commander general John J. Pershing gathered his divisions together to form the 1st American Army and began his own offensive. The American troops fought with an enthusiasm that incited contemptuous remarks

from the French and British soldiers, and often panic from the Germans.

In the hundred days following the beginning of the offensive, the French, British and Americans took 363,000 prisoners, a quarter of the German army in the west, and seized 6,400 guns, half their total number. The troops and cannons remaining were not enough even to defend the German borders. On 28 September Ludendorff lost his nerve, screaming in such desperation in his office in the Spa headquarters that the officers closed the doors. He then told General Field Marshal Hindenburg that a ceasefire had to be agreed at once. But Hindenburg and Ludendorff did not want to do that off their own bats. Ludendorff wrote that the politicians and Reichstag representatives must 'lie in the bed they themselves had made,' as if they had lost their nerve in the face of the Allied attacks. On 3 October 1918, Kaiser Wilhelm named Prince Max von Baden as the new Reichskanzler, known to the Allies for his moderate nature. He telegraphed the Allies that very same day, requesting a ceasefire.

German soldiers reading newspapers on the eastern front. The headlines are the same, day after day. Today: 'Good situation in East and West'.

(*Opposite*) The Austro-Hungarian General Staff on the eastern front. After four years, in the autumn of 1918 the Austro-Hungarian army is no longer fit for combat.

Prince Max von Baden was familiar with Ludendorff's devious ways, so had made sure he had Hindenburg's written confirmation that it was impossible to 'force peace upon the enemy'. But that did not help. For as soon as Prince Max and the centrist parties of the Reichstag had offered negotiations to the Allies, Ludendorff acted as though he had nothing to do with the defeat. Instead, he claimed that the troops would have fought on if they hadn't been held back by the politicians. Even the German officers were disgusted by this. The leader of the Mürwik marine school in Flensburg, Captain Christoph Moritz von Egidy, called it 'unmanly and above all ignoble, when one is completely ruined (as we are) and has had to retreat from the stage, to consistently try to put a spanner in the works for the opponent, particularly when

A boy sitting outside the church of the East Prussian town of Muschaken. The battle of Tannenberg took place in the immediate vicinity.

they stepped in during a moment of danger. For we are, indeed, completely ruined'.

By now, Germany's ally, Austria-Hungary, had fallen apart. On 6 October, the Serbian, Croatian and Slovenian subjects of the Danubian monarchy proclaimed their participation in the founding of a South Slav state, and a day later Poland announced the reformation of the Polish state in the Habsburg, Russian and German regions. On 28 October, the Czechoslovakian Republic was proclaimed in Prague. On 1 November, the government of an independent Hungary was formed in Budapest. Now the German-occupied countries between Bodensee and Neusiedler See stood alone, and signed a truce on 3 November.

That was also the day when the German revolution began. The marine officers who had spent almost the entire war in the casinos decided to carry out one last heroic act, by challenging the Royal Navy to a decisive battle. On 30 October, the order rang out to prepare the ships for one last deployment. The sailors mutinied, broke into the armouries and went armed on to the streets. By 3 November, they had captured Kiel. The general inspector of the marines, Prince Heinrich of Prussia, disguised himself and fled the city the following day. His brother, Kaiser Wilhelm, had already left Berlin on 29 October and had hastened to Spa in Belgium, where the German army headquarters were still located. On 8 November, Kurt Eisner formed a new government in Munich, and the following day Prince Max von Baden surrendered the Reich Chancellery to Friedrich Ebert, the leader of the Social Democrats.

In Spa, Kaiser Wilhelm consulted with his officers as to whether he should deploy the army against the people. General Field Marshal Hindenburg listened in silence and deferred the response to the moderate General Wilhelm Groener, who knew from a survey of fifty regiment commanders that all the soldiers wanted was for the war to end. They would no longer obey an order to fight their own people in Germany. When the Kaiser reminded him that the troops had taken an oath to the flag and to him as supreme commander, Groener answered him by saying: 'An oath to the flag? Supreme commander? Those are mere words now.' The following day, Wilhelm boarded the train to Holland and retreated to his castle in Doorn. On his arrival, he asked for a 'cup of good English tea'.

On 11 November 1918, the German ceasefire delegation signed a treaty in the French headquarters in Compiègne. The war was over, but without peace having been won. What had been proven, according to the interpretation of British historian Charles Cruttwell in 1934, was that war between the modern great states was no longer an 'instrument of politics', like in Carl von Clausewitz's day. 'It is inevitably becoming a battle for existence in which there are no more limits regarding the use of people and money,' he wrote, 'in which aims can no longer be clearly defined and peace cannot be attained through rapprochement.'

Inside a German officers' dugout on the western front in Belgium. At the end of the war many dugouts are constructed from prefabricated concrete elements.

As the situation for Germany worsens, the more people suffer from food shortages and the ongoing strains of conflict, and so Fuhrmann's Kaiserpanoramas begin to make less and less money. The war has gone on for too long and people have sacrificed too much to pay to see the illusion of heroic war. The last datable series in Fuhrmann's collection before the war ends – the visit of Kaiser Wilhelm II and Charles I in the conquered Italian territories – does not portray glorious conquerors, but only weary, emaciated men.

Austria, c. 1916. Medical examination of 'wrecks'. As the war drags on, front soldiers resort to every possible means to escape the inferno of the battles.

"The deputy commander-in-chief of the 2nd Army Corps noticed a decline in discipline, and saw the chief reason for this as lying in the failure of the NCOs. The deputy commander-in-chief of the 4th Army Corps reported a considerable increase in absence without leave from the end of March, and an increase in punishable actions with the obvious goal of escaping the front. The deputy commander-in-chief of the 10th Army Corps reported that among non-seriously wounded men numbering 594, only 217 could be described as mildly ill. Many of the shirkers went into the big cities to go into hiding there. At the end of June the deputy commander-in-chief of the 5th Army Corps reported on the poisonous influence of the Russian refuseniks, not only on the infantry reserves, but also on the civilian population. There had been problems transporting several hundred men to the west. They had to be located far apart because of the danger of mutiny before then being taken away in individual transports."

**Erich Otto Volkmann,
German general staff officer**

Brest-Litovsk, Russia, December 1917. In the October Revolution, the Bolsheviks under Lenin seize power. To consolidate their power they have to make peace with Germany and Austria. At the peace conference of Brest-Litovsk the Russian delegation has to hand over enormous amounts of territory – that is the German price of peace in the east.

"We crossed the line, preceded by a trumpeter carrying a white flag. Three hundred yards from the German entanglements we were met by German officers.

At five o'clock, our eyes blindfolded, we were conducted to a battalion staff of the German army, where we handed over our written authorization from the National Commissaries to two officers of the German General Staff, who had been sent for the purpose.

The negotiations were conducted in the French language. Our proposal to carry on negotiations for an armistice on all the fronts of belligerent countries, in order later to make peace, was immediately handed over to the staff of the division, whence it was sent by direct wire to the staff commander of the eastern front and to the chief commander of the German armies.

At 6.20 we were taken in a motor car to the minister's house on the road from Dvinsk to Ponevezh, where we were received by Divisional General von Hoffmeister, who informed us that our proposal had been handed to the highest commander, and that a reply probably would be received in twenty-four hours.

But at 7.30 the first answer from the chief of the general command already had been received, announcing agreement to our proposals, and leaving the details of the next meeting to General von Hoffmeister and the Parliamentarians."

Lev Kamenev, Bolshevik Russian delegate

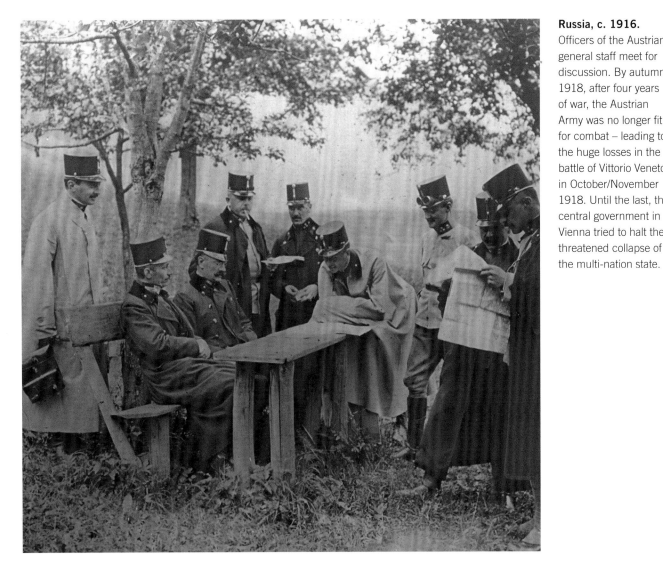

Russia, c. 1916. Officers of the Austrian general staff meet for discussion. By autumn 1918, after four years of war, the Austrian Army was no longer fit for combat – leading to the huge losses in the battle of Vittorio Veneto in October/November 1918. Until the last, the central government in Vienna tried to halt the threatened collapse of the multi-nation state.

"When a doctor has to perform a difficult operation, and people are standing behind him with their watches in their hands and forcing him to complete the operation in a few minutes, then the operation might conclude with a world speed record, but the patient will thank the doctor afterwards for the manner of its execution. If you awaken the fundamentally incorrect impression amongst our contemporary adversaries that we have to finish things off at any cost and straight away, we won't get 100,000 kilograms of grain, and the success will be a more Platonic one."

Ottokar Czernin, foreign secretary of Austria-Hungary, during the First World War, in his *Appell an das Hinterland*, as revolutions sparked by the still-ongoing war were tearing apart the age-old empire

Cetinje, Montenegro, 1916. From the very start of the war, comparatively small Serbia seems to have no chance against the army of Austria-Hungary. But the Serbs stop all Austrian attacks, and frustrate the strategies of the Central Powers. Only the invasion of Bulgaria, which turns the Serbian battlefield into a war on two fronts, leads to the definitive defeat of Serbia and Montenegro in 1916.

"King Nikita's double game is over. The whole of Montenegro is occupied by Austrians; the army is disarmed. The Montenegrin people are completely weary of war and have only one desire: bread! The Montenegrins will receive their peace, even without their king, who has faithlessly abandoned them in their darkest hour. In the west there are big battles, prisoners, captured war materials again. Waited in vain for a message from Kurt. And still nothing about peace!"

Elisabeth Kreiter, German soldier's mother

▶ **Gorizia, Italy, 1917.** In October 1917, in the Battle of Caporetto, Austria-Hungary and Germany succeed in making an unprecedented breakthrough on the Italian front. Emperor Charles I and Kaiser Wilhelm II, shown here on a hill near Gorizia, visit the conquered territories shortly afterwards. The offensive is only halted at the River Piave, because supplies cannot be brought so far into enemy territory.

"Mama was with Frau Frey in Karlsruhe, shopping. How different it must have been in the elegant little residence. The opulent copper decorations at the station have disappeared, the shops are bleak and empty, even down to the meagre shop window displays, you don't get anything to eat or anything to drink, and in the railway carriages it is dark and cold. Travelling is certainly no pleasure. But our triumphal procession in Italy is advancing inexorably."

Elisabeth Kreiter, German soldier's mother

Montfaucon, France, c. 1916. Exhausted German officers planning in a dugout. With the capitulation of Austria-Hungary on 3 November 1918, Germany finds itself facing the superior power of the Allies on its own. With the prospect of total defeat on the horizon, German supreme command requests a ceasefire on 11 November 1918.

"I realize gradually that all the land round us on all sides is a warren with Germans in small parties hiding in it, not yet 'mopped up'. Our NZ cavalryman comes back with three new captives, and I march off my little flock of seven. Nevinson questions them fluently in German and they agree, with expressive gestures, that 'they are fed up to the teeth with war'."

C.E. Montague, British war correspondent

Aquileia, Italy, 1917. Kaiser Wilhelm visits a village cemetery in conquered Aquileia. After the disastrous defeat at Caporetto the Italian army spends a year rebuilding. The hated commander Luigi Cadorna is dismissed and the last reserves are called in. After the exertion of Caporetto, Austria can barely mobilize any more troops.

"I let the old man go on talking while Liesbeth and I read the latest bulletins: 'Count Karolyi was yesterday appointed Prime Minister by the Emperor. Count Karolyi has recalled the Hungarian regiments from the Italian Front. Count Tisza has been shot by two soldiers.' A second Extra Edition brought the war bulletin: 'On the Italian Mountain Front our troops will systematically carry out the proposed measures of evacuation and occupy the same positions as at the beginning of the Italian campaign. In the Venetian plain the retreat across the Tagliamento is in progress. The total evacuation of Serbian territory is about to be effected.' Liesbeth and I were plunged in consternation. What was going to happen? We had no soldiers to spare. How could we replace the Hungarian regiments? We could not replace them; that the bulletin made quite clear. Retreat all along the Italian and Serbian Front. We tried to reassure and comfort each other, but were both filled with secret apprehension."

Anna Eisenmenger, middle-class Austrian woman in Vienna

Verdun, France, November 1918. As a result of Germany's unlimited U-boat war, to which many American ships fall victim, the United States is drawn into the war in 1917. It takes almost a year for larger American units to appear on the western front but here, too, the US applies its economic power in favour of entente.

Gorizia, Italy, 1917. Emperor Charles I and Kaiser Wilhelm II in the citadel of the conquered town of Gorizia. In June 1918 Austria-Hungary, using its very last reserves, launches one last attack on the Italian front. But the Italian army, led by the capable General Armando Diaz, fights off the assaults.

"I hope everybody at home knows what a splendid thing the Americans did (it was published in the English papers some days ago) in agreeing to put in a lot of their troops to serve as parts of larger British and French units. One has to know the inside of an army to appreciate all the postponement of personal and national self-love and ambition that it meant. It may have sounded merely technical, but it was really one of the greatest acts of chivalry of the war."

C.E. Montague, British war correspondent

"The intoxication of war has fled, no one is volunteering any more, enthusiasm is being drummed into the young recruits, almost children, ill-fed and feeble. In their patriotic training they are being told they must learn that Germany has a right to Belgium, to the Baltic provinces, to colonies. But they don't listen to the words of well-fed orators, they listen to the rumours that one passes on to the next, that regiments at the front are supposed to have mutinied, Austria won't be able to hold out for long, in this place or that women have been looting bakeries and butchers' shops. Soldiers are already refusing to go into the field, the officers have to struggle to persuade them, punishments don't scare them. 'Better to starve in jail than perish outside,' one of them called when he was being arrested."

Ernst Toller, German poet and soldier

Gorizia, Italy, 1917. Emperor Charles I and Kaiser Wilhelm II enjoy an alfresco breakfast on the Gorizia citadel. The counter-attack follows in October – it takes the Italian army less than two weeks to annihilate the Austro-Hungarian army. Austria-Hungary, ruled by Emperor Charles I since 1916, collapses when the many nations of the huge empire demand independence and the end of the war.

"Hardship in Germany is growing, the bread is getting worse, the milk thinner, the farmers are chasing the city-dwellers from their farmyards, the scavengers are coming home empty-handed, the soldiers at the front, bitter about the carousals and debauchery of the base, are fed up with the war. 'Same wages, same food, the war would have been forgotten long ago,' sing the soldiers."

Ernst Toller, German poet and soldier

Belgium, c. 1916. Exhausted German officers in their dugout, after a battle. The hundred-day offensive on the western front begins on 8 August 1918. Strengthened by fresh American units and equipped with hundreds of new tanks, the Allies crush the German positions. For Germany, collapse is imminent.

"We may go gratefully into this last day of the old year. Kurt and Lotte are here, and Kurt's boy, who has been looking after him so loyally for two and a half years. Today we just want to be quiet and fold our hands and thank God. And yet there is great chaos in the house, from all the people and all the going in and out. How uplifting it is when Kurt says from outside that they can hardly expect the forthcoming major offensive in the west, how general the enthusiasm is and as great as it was in 1914. How well everything is going out there, Hindenburg and Ludendorff are doing wonderful things. Now may God alone bless their work at the start of the year of peace, 1918."

Elisabeth Kreiter, mother of a German soldier

Swinemünde, Germany, before the war. Sailors aboard a warship sweep the deck, during a peacetime naval manoeuvre. They aren't called upon for much more during the war. When the defeat of the army on the western front is only a matter of time, Wilhelm II decides to send his navy into a decisive battle against Britain, in a last-ditch attempt to win the war. It would be a suicide mission, as the fleet is no match for the Royal Navy. The crews on individual ships in the fleet anchored at Wilhelmshaven refuse to obey the order.

"*Late at night the following telephone call suddenly arrived: 'Here in Cuxhaven the workers' and soldiers' council has formed. Tomorrow at nine there will be a meeting in the parade ground at Grimmerhörn. All military service will stop. Weapons are to be brought. Signature: workers' and soldiers' council.'*

I beckoned over the deputy, Ponarth. We went into the people's bedroom, woke them, and I told them of the telephone call. I was very agitated. 'Go,' I said, 'but if possible don't take guns. Now confer without me.' They did that, and then insisted on taking guns, and also demanded immediate payment of their wages. They also treated me with great kindness and respect."

Joachim Ringelnatz, German sailor and author

▶ **Kiel, Germany, before the war.**
Sailors and workers in Kiel demand 'Peace and Bread'. Kiel garrison joins the rebels – and on the evening of 4 November 1918, the city is firmly in their hands. The revolution spreads from here across the whole of Germany.

"The sailors of the fleet, the Kaiser's blue boys, are the first to revolt. The High Seas fleet is to leave harbour, the officers prefer 'defeat in honour to shameful peace'. The sailors, who were pioneers of the revolution as early as 1917, refuse, they turn off the fires for the engines, six hundred men are arrested, the sailors leave the ships, storm the prisons, take over the city of Kiel, the dock workers join them and the German revolution has begun."

Ernst Toller, German poet and soldier

Istanbul, before the war. The navy is the pride of Wilhelm II – but during the war, apart from the battle of Skagerrak, it stays in the harbour. After the refusal of the order off Wilhelmshaven the German battleships are ordered back to Kiel. Here the dock workers join the sailors in open mutiny.

"Suddenly the door was pushed open with a loud crash. Two big sailors, with rifles in their hands, their faces deathly white, stood in the doorway. One of them called out, 'We are delegates of the soldiers' council. There are no superiors any more! There is no saluting any more!' I gave them the keys, including the ones to the ammunition room and gave them something to eat, because they had come a long way and were also exhausted from their inner agitation. Now they sat down at my table. Some of the people from Seeheim joined us. The delegates made a sympathetic impression, particularly Kraus, the carpenter from Stickenbüttel. They calmly told me that everything had gone well. The soldiers' council was determined to stick to the strictest orders. They wanted immediate peace at any price. Officers were also allowed to appear at the meeting, but they were forbidden to bring weapons along. Some officers, for example Patronenmüller, had been talked about in very threatening terms. They had to leave town immediately."

Joachim Ringelnatz, German sailor and author

"*On 9 November 1918 the Berlin workers leave their factories, from the east, south and north the masses move to the centre of the city, old grey-haired men, women who have spent years at the lathes of the ammunition factories, war wounded, cripples, students, office workers. The time of the uprising was not determined by leaders, the revolutionary representatives had expected a later day, the constitutional socialist MPs are surprised and shocked, they were engaged in negotiations with Reich Chancellor Prinz Max von Baden to save the Hohenzollern monarchy.*"

Ernst Toller, German poet and soldier

Nantillois, France, c. 1916. Obedient German soldiers pose with a statue of their supreme commander, Emperor Wilhelm II. By the autumn of 1918, Wilhelm can no longer be sure of their obedience. Wilhelm learns about the Berlin revolution while in Spa, in Belgium, where the German supreme command is based. His generals tell him they have lost control of the army. On the morning of 10 November he travels to the Dutch border and asks to be interned.

"There has been much talk of me leaving the army and going to a neutral country abroad. Some say: the Kaiser should have gone to a unit at the front, joined it in attacking the enemy and sought death in one last attack. But not only would that have made impossible the armistice so hotly desired by the people, and for which the commission already dispatched from Berlin to General Foch was negotiating, but the lives of many soldiers, and the best and most loyal, would have been pointlessly sacrificed.

Still others say: the Kaiser should have taken his own life. That was ruled out by my firm Christian perspective. And would they not then have said: 'How cowardly! Now he is shaking off all responsibility by committing suicide.' That way out was also rendered impossible because I had to be able to help and serve my people and my country in the difficult time that was bound to lie ahead."

Wilhelm II, after the war

France, 1917. In October 1918 there are still German troops in Belgium and France, and no Entente soldier has set foot on German soil, but the war has been lost for good. On 11 November the armistice is signed in a railway carriage in Compiègne.

"About nine, in the G office of VIII Corps, I get the news that the war is to be over at eleven this morning. With all speed we go through Valenciennes towards Mons, which we know was in enemy's hands last night. E. of Jemappes a big crater in the road stops us, but I find a way round through Cuesmes and we motor into Mons at eleven to the moment. Many aeroplanes flying low over the front lines dropping signal flares. The only German we see as we go into Mons is a dead one lying under the boulevard trees. As we go in, the streets are crowded with civilians, cheering and waving flags and shouting English words to us."

C.E. Montague, British war correspondent

The battlecruiser *Seydlitz*, c. 1915. In line with the conditions of the armistice, the German fleet is interned at Scapa Flow, Scotland. To keep the German ships from falling into the hands of the Allies, the commanding admiral, Ludwig von Reuter, orders the fleet to be scuttled on 21 June 1919. Nine sailors and officers die – the last casualties of the First World War.

"The Friedrich der Grosse *listed far over, streams of water poured inside through the open windows – another few minutes, it capsizes and sinks to the depths, the air coming out of the funnels sends up two great sprays of water – then all is still, a few remnants drift on the abandoned cemetery. It is sixteen minutes past twelve."*

Ludwig von Reuter, German Admiral of the interned fleet

Kiel, Germany, before the war. Kaiser Wilhelm, in full ceremonial dress, surveys a model of the victory column before the war. In November 1918, after the bloodiest war in human history has raged across the world for four and a half years, his certainty of victory has turned into certainty of the demise of his ruling house. On 28 November – nineteen days after the proclamation of the Republic in Germany – Kaiser Wilhelm abdicates. He hopes by doing so to stabilize the situation in the Reich and prevent a civil war.

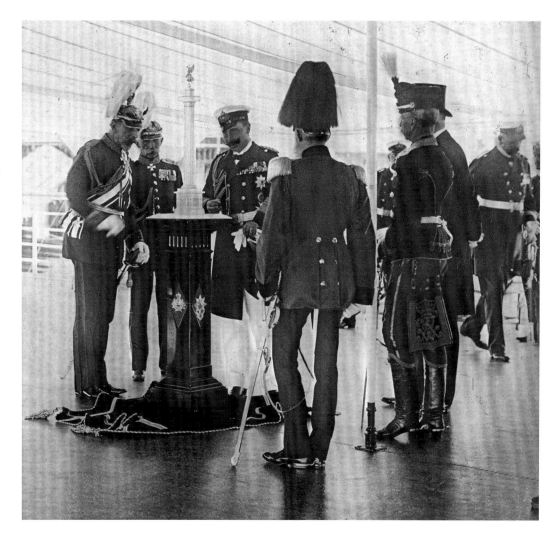

"*I hereby renounce for all time the rights to the throne of Prussia and to the German Imperial throne therewith connected.*

At the same time I release all officials of the German Empire and of Prussia, as well as all officers, non-commissioned officers and men of the navy and of the Prussian army, as well as the troops of the federated states of Germany, from the oath of fidelity which they tendered to me as their Emperor, King and Commander-in-Chief.

I expect of them that until the re-establishment of order in the German Empire they shall render assistance to those in actual power in Germany, in protecting the German people from the threatening dangers of anarchy, famine, and foreign rule.

Proclaimed under our own hand and with the Imperial seal attached.
Amerongen, 28 November 1918."

Wilhelm II

August Fuhrmann with one of his cameras.

AUGUST FUHRMANN AND THE KAISERPANORAMA

In 1911, German author Franz Kafka journeyed to Friedland in northern Bohemia and came across an example of the Kaiserpanorama – August Fuhrmann's remarkable invention for displaying stereoscopic glass slides. Kafka was taken aback, not having expected to find 'such a beautiful device' on his travels. Though public fascination in the major cities of Europe, such as Prague, had long since moved on from Fuhrmann's machine to the newly invented cinematograph, Kafka was truly taken with it, describing it as the 'sole pleasure' available in Friedland. 'I had forgotten the set up of the panorama and, for a moment, feared I would have to go from one chair to the next,' the author wrote. 'An old man at a small candlelit table, reading an edition of *Illustrierte Welt*, conducted the whole thing… At the end I wanted to tell him how much I had enjoyed it, but didn't pluck up the courage. I picked up the next programme. Open from ten in the morning until ten at night.'

It was in the 1870s that August Fuhrmann (1844–1925) came up with the idea of having stereoscopic pictures rotate within a carousel to create a three-dimensional effect. Up to twenty-five viewers at a time were able to sit around the circular wooden construction and, through viewing lenses, see fifty hand-painted glass slides in each programme, rotating inside the device. The pictures were illuminated from the rear by petroleum or gas lighting, which was intermittently extinguished. The philosopher Walter Benjamin, born in 1892, had fond memories of the Kaiserpanorama from his Berlin childhood: 'A defect in the illumination suddenly caused that rare dusk in which the colour disappeared from the landscape. Then it lay there silently under an ashen sky; it was as though I could have heard the wind and the bells if I had only listened more closely.'

For Fuhrmann, the showcasing of pictures such as this became a calling. In truth, it had been one ever since he had seen 'dissolving pictures' as a young man. In these, two projectors displayed on a four-metre square surface pictures of landscapes or cities (or even paintings) captured in both summer and winter. Then one image was gradually 'dissolved' while the other was superimposed. This created the illusion of the seasons changing before the viewer's eyes. A third projector was able to bring movement into the pictures, creating snow or rainfall, volcanic eruptions, sunrise or sunset. Bright light for the projections was created with limelight, a phosphor or hydrogen gas, and oxygen. It was quite common for there to be an explosion, bringing the presentation to an end with dramatic effect.

As a young man, Fuhrmann bought himself a 'gioskop', a triple projector, and set off on tour. 'The eye is the door to the soul; beauty and goodness provide the key,' he proclaimed. The theatre rooms he performed in were often filled to the very last seat. Before long, he had earned enough money to leave this aspect of his work, concentrating instead on stereoscopy and a particular project. By 1880 he had created a new device, which he presented in Breslau. He was already calling it the 'Kaiserpanorama', even though he hadn't received the Kaiser's permission to do so. Fuhrmann was an experienced entrepreneur. He knew that his 'Glass Stereo Series' and 'Observation Apparatus' needed a catchy name: 'The next task was to find a name for the device I'd created. I hardly need to emphasize how important it is to find the appropriate term for such an endeavour, something which is destined to be in the public domain for both young and old. From all the names I considered, Kaiserpanorama was the one I chose.'

Stereoscopic 3-D photography was already well developed in the 1880s. Colour photography, on the other hand, was still the preserve of a few amateurs experimenting at home with emulsions and colour filters. That's why Fuhrmann focused on hand-coloured pictures for his Kaiserpanoramas. He had the corresponding colours painted on the rear side of the glass positives, so that a colour picture appeared when light shone through. Fuhrmann took the precise secrets of this colouring process with him to the grave. Even today, all we know is that he employed porcelain painters who coloured each picture individually.

In time, people all over Germany and throughout Europe became familiar with Fuhrmann's Kaiserpanorama. For the first few years, he only exhibited his original device, taking it from Breslau to Frankfurt in 1882, and then on to Berlin in 1883. After that, numerous branches were established. Fuhrmann provided the demonstration models, and from then on the branch owners worked independently. Before long, other manufacturers were supplying devices that also operated with Fuhrmann's picture slides. By 1910, there were 250 branches across Europe, with 100,000 glass slides in circulation; these were frequently extended with new themes. The First World War offered plenty of material for new cycles, and around fifty picture cycles were produced across all the fronts. Fuhrmann himself, by then seventy years old, even photographed on the western front. The wartime images were often shown in special demonstrations known as the 'war panoramas'.

Furhmann was a successful entrepreneur, but also saw himself as a teacher. He lent small presentation devices to schools and clubs, and also supplied presentation manuscripts. Acoustic programmes with presentations and musical accompaniment became widespread. Kaiser Wilhelm II was very taken by the use of this multimedia concept and commissioned Fuhrmann with the documentation of memorable events, for example the opening of the Kiel Canal in 1895, the annual sailing event Kiel Week (which Wilhelm regularly participated in), Wilhelm II's Oriental journey in 1898, and the funeral procession of Wilhelm's mother, the Princess Royal, in 1901. The Kaiser himself was quite the media star, and very much admired by Fuhrmann. As 'court supplier', he even supplied the Kaiser with his own coloured glass plates. At the inauguration of the Kiel Canal, the Kaiser selected a hundred glass stereos to be inserted into the capstone in Holtenau. Fuhrmann's photographs were deposited in the plinths of the Berlin memorials for Kaiser Wilhelm I, Kaiser Friedrich III and Field Marshal Helmuth von Moltke [the Elder]. Fuhrmann was particularly proud of this: 'For future historical research, my glass stereos have achieved meaning, regardless of what other documents might outlive them.'

The important historical documents created by Furhmann include photographs of rooms in Kaiser Wilhelm's palaces, the living quarters of the Ottoman Sultan in the old seraglio in Istanbul, and even pictures of the Sultan Mehmed V himself. Pope Leo XIII gave Fuhrmann, a Protestant, access to his private living quarters, where he was able to photograph the furniture, artistic treasures and his Holiness himself.

Even before the First World War, the cinema screen had begun to lure the public away from panoramas. Fuhrmann succeeded in reviving the 3-D euphoria with his pictures from the fronts during the war, but when both the conflict and the imperial period came to an end, the public lost interest.

After having been so inventive and innovative for many decades, Fuhrmann didn't get involved in the new medium of film, even though his experience would have served him very well. For the dimming, blending and manipulating of his 'dissolving pictures', he was already using a technique which would later be used in film. Even the picture series and cutting techniques of film had their roots in the picture stories of the panorama carousel. But feeling that he had to defend his 3-D pictures, Fuhrmann fought in vain against the cinemas.

For a long time, the Kaiserpanoramas fell largely into obscurity. The only Kaiserpanorama to have stayed in place from the beginning of the twentieth century until today is the Fotoplastikon in Warsaw. After the Second World War, museums searched for the few projection devices still in existence and began to exhibit them. Today, original Kaiserpanoramas are once again attracting visitors both young and old, for example in the German Historical Museum and the City Museum in Berlin, and in the Media Culture House in Wels. The era of the most delicate panorama is not over, because its magic can still work alongside other mediums.

INDEX

Note: page numbers in **bold** refer to information contained in captions.

ACKNOWLEDGEMENTS

We would like to express our thanks to Annelen Karge and the Cultural History Museum of Rostock for sharing August Fuhrmann's wonderful photographs, Manfred Jehle for his excellent collaboration on the historical texts, French photographer Emile Taudière for the images from the French side of the front, to his grandson Laurent Duret for his generous support, to Bertl Strasser for trusting us with the drawings of his grandfather Karl Kasser, to Henrik Sucher, Marlen Müssiggang and Günter Dedio for their help in finding the best quotations, to Professor Dr Oliver Janz and Yury Winterberg for sharing their inexhaustable knowledge about the First World War, to Niko Vialkowitsch for his infectious enthusiasm for, and limitless knowledge of, stereoscopes, and to Sue Temple and Barbara Wenner for their expert advice.

This book is published to accompany the television series entitled *The Great War Diaries*, produced by LOOKS Distribution GmbH and first broadcast on BBC Two in 2014.

Produced by: Gunnar Dedio
Directed by: Jan Peter
Commissioning Editor for the BBC: Carol Sennett

10 9 8 7 6 5 4 3 2 1

Published in 2014 by BBC Books, an imprint of Ebury Publishing. A Random House Group Company.

© LOOKS Distribution GmbH 2014
Foreword © Peter Englund 2014

The Random House Group Limited Reg. No. 954009

Addresses for companies within the Random House Group can be found at www.randomhouse.co.uk

A CIP catalogue record for this book is available from the British Library.

ISBN: 978 1 84990 674 6

The Random House Group Limited supports the Forest Stewardship Council® (FSC®), the leading international forest-certification organisation. Our books carrying the FSC label are printed on FSC®-certified paper. FSC is the only forest-certification scheme supported by the leading environmental organisations, including Greenpeace. Our paper procurement policy can be found at www.randomhouse.co.uk/environment

Commissioning editor: Albert DePetrillo
Project editor: Joe Cottington
Copy editor: Bernice Davison
Translators: Shaun Whiteside, Jamie Lee Searle, Nicholas Caistor, Ruth Martin, Geoffrey Mulligan and Richard Dixon
Design: O'Leary & Cooper
Production: Phil Spencer

Printed and bound by Firmengruppe APPL, aprinta druck, Wemding, Germany

To buy books by your favourite authors and register for offers visit
www.randomhouse.co.uk